GUNPOWDER ARTILLERY

1600 – 1700

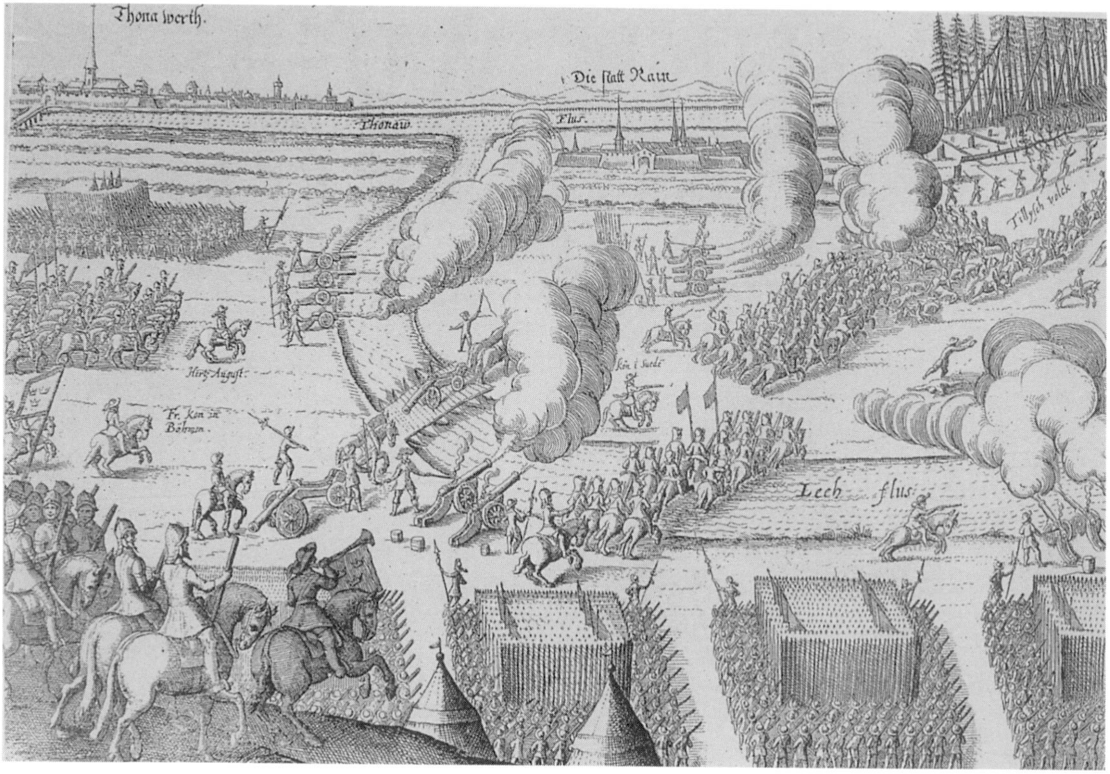
Thona werth
Die statt Rain
Thonaw
Flus
Tillysch volck
Hertz August
Kön i Suede
Fr. Kön in
Böhmen
Lech flus

GUNPOWDER ARTILLERY

1600 – 1700

John Norris

The Crowood Press

First published in 2005 by
The Crowood Press Ltd
Ramsbury, Marlborough
Wiltshire SN8 2HR

www.crowood.com

British Library Cataloguing-in-Publication Data
A catalogue record for this book is available from the British Library.

ISBN 1 86126 691 X

Typeset by NBS Publications, Basingstoke, Hampshire, RG21 5NH

Printed and bound in Great Britain by CPI Bath

Contents

	Dedication and Acknowledgements	6
	Introduction	7
1	The Beginning of a New Era: 1600–1625	9
2	The Years 1626–1650	25
3	The Years 1651–1675	35
4	The Years 1676–1700	47
5	Japan and the Far East	66
6	Russia and Eastern Europe	73
7	The English Civil War	77
8	Barrel Casting	100
9	Naval Artillery	110
10	Tools and the Artillery Train	127
11	The Gunners and Printed Books	149
	Bibliography	156
	Index	157

DEDICATION

This work is dedicated to my daughter Charlotte April Norris in the year of her twenty-first birthday. She, too, has heard the thunder of guns ancient and modern.

ACKNOWLEDGEMENTS

I would like to extend my sincere gratitude to the various historical re-enactment groups portraying the seventeenth century. They gave freely of their time, and allowed me to photograph the weapons of the seventeenth century, which they have faithfully recreated. I am also most grateful to all staff at the various historical sites who were most courteous and helpful at all stages of this work. Without the support, dedication and hard work of such people we would not know as much as we do today.

Introduction

The Italian General Raimondo Montecuccoli stated that: 'For war you need three things: 1 Money: 2 Money: 3 Money.' He was absolutely correct, because as events were to prove in the seventeenth century, wars were becoming increasingly costly to wage, both financially and in terms of man-power. This was never more self-evident than in the branch of artillery. Artillery was given the distinctive title 'Ultima ratio regum', which translates into 'The last argument of kings'. This should also include emperors, for they too, along with monarchs, were the figures with whom artillery became most associated: it was the kings, emperors and other heads of state who could afford to pay for the deployment of such weaponry on the battlefield.

From the seventeenth century onwards wars absorbed more men, and became more intense and, as the armies grew larger, more sophisticated. As the historian Christopher Duffy points out: 'You had to think in terms of decades or generations if you wished to form your construction engineers and gunners, assemble powerful siege trains, and win and consolidate frontiers.' Certainly it took time to change years of indoctrination and forge new armies that would be inculcated with the new military theories. Some military commanders had a forceful nature and brought about this change rapidly, such as King Gustavus Adolphus of Sweden, and Oliver Cromwell who founded the New Model Army during the English Civil War.

Wars in the seventeenth century were fought on a scale never before thought possible. The Hundred Years War had been protracted, but the distances across which wars in this century were fought were staggering. Armies grew in size, and the battlefield – that is to say, the overall size – also increased in depth and width as weapons, especially artillery, became more powerful and increased in range. The main reason for this was artillery that was used in virtually every action, large and small, on land and at sea. At the Battle of Breitenfeld on 17 September 1631 each side deployed around 40,000 troops, and the opening artillery bombardment lasted some two hours. The battle developed and was hard fought, but it was artillery that made its presence felt. The Swedish batteries fired more rapidly than those of the Austrian army, which in the end fled the battlefield, leaving behind several thousand dead and about the same number taken prisoner.

Artillery changed during this period and evolved into new designs, but at a slower and more radical rate than previously. The artillery train was also transformed so that it could keep pace with the army on the march. For example, in 1625 the Swedish artillery train of only thirty-six guns required 1,000 horses and 220 wagons and carts. Only five years later this had been refined and improved so that eighty pieces of artillery still required 1,000 horses, but only one hundred wagons and carts. After 1660 the actual design of artillery pieces changed very little, and it remained virtually unaltered for the next 150 years. What would make the difference was the way in which artillery was deployed on the battlefield, and how it was used to engage the enemy. Some existing types of artillery, such as mortars, were used to greater effect, especially at sieges, and new types of ammunition were introduced.

A number of scientific improvements were introduced in the seventeenth century, not all of which had a direct military application. Those inventions that could be used by the military to their advantage were seized on and used to great effect. In this era nations carved out the beginnings of empires, and small states fought for their very survival. Science provided the gunners with a greater understanding of the weapons they used, which in turn led to more experimentation and future improvement. Warfare had changed with the advent of artillery: during the seventeenth century there were just as many wars and battles fought as ever before, but they were more destructive. There were sieges of cities and castles, all involving the use of artillery. For this reason, it is impossible to include all the battles that were influenced by the presence of artillery during the fighting; instead, it is only practicable to list those battles and sieges where artillery made a significant contribution to the outcome.

Warfare was on the brink of change from which there would be no turning back: the military leaders of the day would take their armies forward and lay the foundations for even further developments in the future. Artillery, once seen as a cumbersome burden that had to be hauled laboriously to the battlefield, was transformed into a highly mobile branch of the army: from being a static weapon on the battlefield, during this period commanders used this new-found versatility to move it about the battlefield to give fire support wherever needed. This period also saw the final disappearance of the archer and pikeman or halberdier from the battlefield. An often quoted statement attributed to Blaise Monluc runs to the effect: 'Il fait plus de peur, que du mal', which translates into 'It frightens more than it hurts'. By the end of the century the days when firearms and artillery merely scared the horses would be long gone. New tactics deployed these weapons in combination, and used them with a scientific application.

1 The Beginning of a New Era: 1600–1625

By 1600, gunpowder artillery had been deployed by armies for some 275 years: it was positively recorded in a manuscript dated around 1326, and since that time, was used in many hundreds of battles across the then known world. The great power of this new weaponry was continuously being improved, and it was only natural that soldiers were keen to test it in battle. The seventeenth century became a period of great change as armies grew in size and advances were made in weapon technology, and battlefield tactics changed accordingly to meet these developments. Again, armies were keen to put such theories to the test and prove the efficacy of the gun drills and the stalwartness of their gunners. Most, if not all these changes, it could be said, dated back to the second half of the sixteenth century. The historian Michael Roberts considered this period to be a 'military revolution', and on this point wrote: 'The perennial problem of tactics: the problem of how to combine missile weapons with close action; how to unite hitting-power, mobility and defensive strength.' He was, of course, correct, but in the seventeenth century only one man, Gustavus Adolphus, the king of Sweden, would come anywhere near to attaining all those points considered to be so important by Michael Roberts.

At the start of this new century the size of artillery forces was increasing across Europe, and this was a trend that would be maintained – indeed, few countries could afford to ignore this fact if they valued their democracy. By the end of the century artillery was being deployed on the battlefield with a more logical approach to the enemy's dispositions, and in the space of one hundred years artillery tactics changed dramatically. Military tacticians grouped guns together in batteries, and tasked them with firing on specific targets. Artillery also provided fire support to other branches of the army in battle, including the infantry as it advanced across the battlefield and supported the sweeping cavalry charges. Much later, these tasks became referred to as 'fire missions', but the object was always to provide support. This century therefore brought a great sweep of change, and where once it was quite sufficient to place two or three guns around the battlefield, that notion became a thing of the past.

In the seventeenth century artillery came to be classified by the weight of the projectiles fired, but even so there were those who still used specific names to identify particular categories of weapon. The size of artillery parks and the artillery train when deployed on campaign also increased in size, much to the annoyance of the infantry who had to march along the same muddy, pock-marked roads that had been churned up by the passing of the cavalry and then the artillery. The use of artillery by now was being channelled towards two roles on the battlefield: the heavy guns

A French field gun showing the large wheels fitted to the carriage, which allowed the gunners to manhandle the weapon through muddy conditions. Such large wheels meant the gun could be wheeled about the battlefield very quickly.

were for use in siege operations, and the lighter guns for field operations and for supporting other branches of the army. And as the weaponry of artillery changed, so too did the men who were operating it.

BIGGER ARMIES

The beginning of the seventeenth century would usher in many aspects concerning the development of artillery in all its forms. The first part of the century formed a new period in the history of artillery, particularly in mainland Europe. Educated men came to influence the course of events over the next century, and this led to a reassessment concerning the way in which warfare was viewed. They would bring about changes in the way in which armies and navies engaged one another in battle, both on land and sea. It became obvious to strategists that artillery, wherever used, would have to evolve in order to meet the changing face of warfare. One of the first proponents in a position of authority, and therefore able to instigate changes, was King Henry IV of France, a highly educated man who realized that artillery had enormous potential and accordingly set about exploiting its power.

In 1600 Henry appointed Maximilian de Bethune, Duc de Sully, to the post of Master-

General of France: as such he was responsible for overseeing the establishment of the French artillery force. Under his direction French artillery became better organized, part of his initiative being to create an elite force equipped with 400 specially cast field pieces. In fact, at the time of Bethune's appointment in 1600 the French army only numbered an estimated 15,000 men, but during the century it would continue to expand to meet the demands of war, and by 1670 had doubled in size. During the Dutch War of 1672–78, Michel le Tellier, Marquis de Louvois, was Under-Secretary of State for War to the court of King Louis XIV, and under his jurisdiction the size of the French army further increased to 120,000 men. In order to fight the War of the League of Augsburg, 1688–97, the French army increased three-fold to 360,000, and by the turn of the century it stood at some 400,000, thus becoming one of the largest armies in Europe.

Another advance in its military structure was the raising of a separate Royal Regiment of Artillery, created in 1693. As a way of putting such moves into perspective, these later increases in the size of the army happened at a time when the population of France was about 20,000,000. At the other end of the scale the army of one Prussian state numbered 18,000 men in 1688 and twenty-five years later in 1713 it was just over double that figure, with 40,000 men.

All across Europe armies were becoming larger, a fact that could not be denied nor ignored, thereby putting a great strain on the civilian population who had to pay for their establishment in taxes. Even the smaller states could not afford to ignore the fact. The Prussian state of Brandenburg during the seventeenth century would increase the size of its army more than eighty-eight fold, from only 900 men to 80,000 men within the space of one hundred years. The justification for having such large armies was that they were required to protect the borders and the populace from a potentially aggressive neighbouring state that might have designs to invade. The military was entering a new age, with governments forming ministerial posts and war offices to manage the conduct of warfare. This age would see professional standing armies being established, within which would be created specialist units such as engineers, but most of all the artillery.

In 1603 Queen Elizabeth, the last monarch of the Tudor dynasty to rule England, died without leaving a direct heir as her successor. King James VI of Scotland was seen as the natural successor, and when he came to the English throne the Stuart Household was established and he ruled the country as King James I. He was deeply interested in military matters, and during the course of his reign between 1603 and 1625 he lent military support to overseas campaigns. James inherited a strong, if somewhat old-fashioned artillery train containing at least eighteen different types of weapon. In addition to this there were many coastal fortifications, built to defend the country from any invasion. These were mainly located to cover harbour installations, and had been the subject of much attention in the immediate aftermath of the Spanish Armada in 1588. But once the danger had passed these fortifications were neglected and in later years were allowed to run down and deteriorate. The artillery at these sites was very often poorly maintained, and many lacked adequate stores of gunpowder and ammunition.

The force may have been Tudor in origin, and some of the gunners were undoubtedly advanced in years, but those facts did not detract from the power the artillery train could bring to the field of battle. However, it was obvious that such a diverse range of weaponry

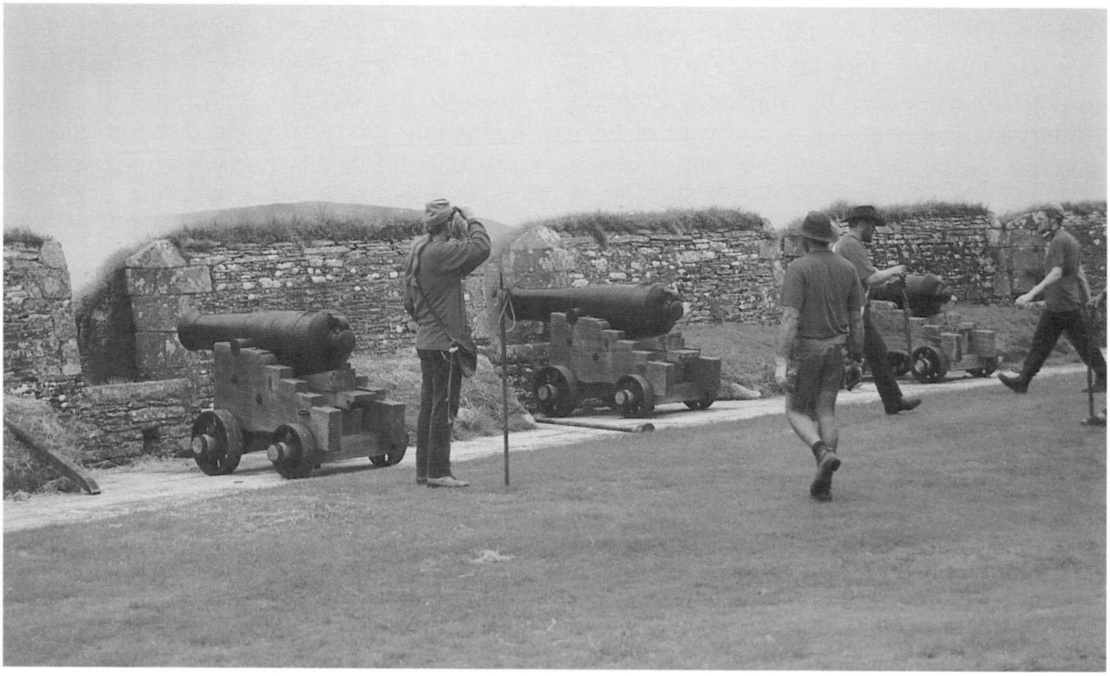

The gun positions at Pendennis Castle in Cornwall. The castle dates back to 1548. During the Civil War it was defended by a Royalist force that mounted artillery in positions such as these.

was not acceptable, simply because of the problems this caused in re-supply. England was not alone in facing this problem, and other European armies were assessing their artillery trains; some were beginning to take drastic action to refine their artillery force. By 1618, fifteen years after his coronation, the organization of the artillery force available to James I included:

> One General of artillery; one Lieutenant of artillery; one Comptroller; one Commissary; ten Gentlemen of artillery; twenty-five Conductors of artillery; one Master gunner; 136 Gunners; one Master fire worker; two Conductors of fire works; two Battery masters; one Petardier; one Master carpenter; twelve carpenters; two Wagon makers; two Gabion makers; two Harness makers; One cooper; two Farriers; one Surgeon; one Surgeon's mate; one Captain of miners; twenty-five miners; one Captain of pioneers; twenty five pioneers; one Trench master; one Wagon master; one Carriage master and one Provost.

All in all this represented a very comprehensive range of skills, which together combined to keep the artillery train and all its aspects in readiness. This formation as it stood in time of peace, cost £20 per day to maintain – but the country still lacked a formal standing army. In time of war the artillery train would expand in size as more wagon drivers and matrosses, gunners' assistants were recruited; and obviously the cost of maintaining the establishment would also rise accordingly.

The list of those men employed to service and maintain the artillery train for James I of England was the same in the artillery trains

A recreated field piece showing the construction of seventeenth-century artillery. Note that the joints between the spokes of the wheel and the felloes have been reinforced to withstand movement over rough ground. The carriage is a heavy design to take the stresses of being towed over long distances and also when fired in battle.

across Europe. Such manpower levels show that this branch of the military had progressed to the point where it warranted its own labour force of skilled artisans. The carpenters and carriage makers were required to build and repair the gun carriages. The engineers and pioneers would construct the gun positions, with farriers responsible for the welfare of the draft horses used to haul the guns. There was a whole host of other services involved in the deployment of artillery, such as blacksmiths to make and repair metal fittings, and rope makers to produce the rope used to haul the guns. All these services supported one another and kept the artillery train functioning. Moreover the organization of such a workforce was being repeated all across Europe as countries established and expanded their branch of artillery.

In 1619 a decree was passed in England that authorized a series of regulations governing the manufacture and sale of artillery. Among these edicts was the fact that only gun foundries in the areas of Kent and Sussex would be given licence to operate. This made sense at the time, for it centralized manufacture, but in later years it would come back to haunt the state. Artillery could only be shipped from the Tower Wharf, and only sold at East Smithfield, a policy that allowed a great deal of control over the sale and movement of weaponry. However, this well-ordered method of gun control would lead to severe repercussions for the Royal Household during the English Civil War, when Parliamentarian forces quickly seized these manufacturing centres and thereby denied the king any replacement weaponry.

JERSEY'S CASTLES

King James wanted to know all about his forces, and ordered that an inventory be prepared itemizing the artillery force within the castles on the island of Jersey. The first to be examined by the king's commissioners was Elizabeth Castle, guarding the southern approaches to the island, which lay within the English territory of the Channel Islands. At the time Jasper Chapman was serving as the Gentleman Porter, under whose orders were a master gunner and his mate, and fifteen other troops to form the garrison. The inventory was

View from one of Elizabeth Castle's gun positions, in St Aubin's Bay on Jersey in the Channel Islands. This is looking across the bay, and provides defence to the harbour in St Helier.

drawn up by the king's commissioners, Sir William Bird and Sir Edward Conway, and dated 6 May 1617. Included on the list of ordnance at the castle were: 'One demi-cannon, two culverins, five demi-culverins, two sakers, one minion, four falcons, three falconets, two perriers and two port-pieces.' The store of ammunition for these guns was impressive, with many hundreds of projectiles along with dozens of barrels of gunpowder.

The castle stands on a rocky promontory in St Aubin's Bay to the south of the island, from where the artillery could cover the approaches to the main anchorage. The castle had been armed with artillery since early Tudor times, and in 1600, when Sir Walter Raleigh became governor of Jersey, the site was well equipped with guns. Over the years it had been subjected to modifications to permit more and improved guns to be sited in defence. It was the formidable appearance of the castle, backed by the potential firepower of the guns, which served as a deterrent to prevent attack. By 1680 an inventory tells us that the armament at the castle had been reduced to four culverins, four demi-culverins, one saker, one cut saker, two murderers and one minion. The castle played a significant role when Parliamentarian forces attacked (*see* Chapter 7, The English Civil War).

Mont Orgueil Castle was the other important defensive site on Jersey, guarding the east coast of the island. The garrison comprised a master gunner and his mate, in addition to nineteen men-at-arms. This is a relatively small garrison, considering the fact that Mont

Mont Orgueil Castle on Jersey in the Channel Islands. An inventory of the castle's artillery by Sir Edward Conway and Sir William Bird in May 1617 shows that the castle was well equipped with ordnance and ammunition.

Another gun platform within Mont Orgueil Castle on the island of Jersey. This position also mounted guns in 1681, including three demi-culverins and one saker.

Gun platform built within the defences of Mont Orgueil Castle on the island of Jersey. This emplacement was equipped with guns during 1681.

Orgueil Castle overlooks the sea lanes between the island and France, which lies only fifteen miles distant. Between 1617 and 1619 the defences at the castle were modified by the addition of ramparts and outer works. The king's commissioners at this site were once more Sir Edward Conway and Sir William Bird, and the inventory they drew up was dated 13 May 1617, only five days after they had completed their work at Elizabeth Castle. The range of artillery they found deployed at Mont Orgueil Castle was comparable to that at Elizabeth Castle and included:

> Brass Ordnance, Mounted- 1 Demi-cannon. 1 Whole Culverin. 1 Demi-Culverin. 2 Falcons. 1 Falconet. Iron Ordnance, Mounted- 1 Demi-Culverin, 6 Sakers. 2 Falcons. 1 Falconet. 1 Mortar. Iron Ordnance, Unserviceable- 2 Mortars. 1 Perrier. 2 Portuguese Basilisks. 4 Fowlers. [The list continues with an inventory of the types of shot available for the guns and includes:] 100 shots of 32-lb for the Demi-Cannon. 200 of 16-lb for the Whole-Culverin. 250 of 9.5-lb for the Demi-Culverin. 300 of 6-lb for the Sakers. 80 of 2-lb for the Falcons. 120 of 1-lb for the Falconets. The shot for the Fowlers weighed 15-lb and there were 180 barrels of powder in the store.

The above list represents quite a disparate arsenal for such a small island; it also reveals how pieces of artillery made of iron and brass were in service at the same time. Furthermore, the fact that some weapons are Portuguese in origin is an indication that artillery was being exported by that country.

Thirteen years later in 1640, just before the outbreak of the English Civil War, a list of artillery held in Mont Orgueil Castle is recorded by the diarist William Prynne as being: 'Fifteen cast pieces of Artillery.' This record indicated that four weapons had been removed, or suggested that either the unserviceable weapons had been taken away or that Prynne did not include these in his account. Exactly forty years later in 1680, Captain Richard Leake, Master Gunner of England prepared '...an accompt taken of all the Ordnance, etc. in Mount Argile Castle'. This was a more complete listing, and actually mentions where each weapon was mounted, being mainly concentrated in the middle ward to protect the castle from attack across the island. At the same time Leake recommended re-arming the castle with two culverins and twenty-two demi-culverins. This meant that only two calibres of projectile would need to be kept in the stores, thereby simplifying re-supply.

MORE ADVANCES

In 1617 a major step forward in military training took place in Holland when John of Nassau established the world's first ever military college. This purpose-built centre of instruction was organized along proper lines to allow the study of lines of communications and logistics. The new military establishment educated students of the military, enabling them to examine the need for better organization in the field, especially as armies continued to increase in size and complexity. However, it was more than one hundred years before other countries began to follow suit. For example England did not establish the Royal Military Academy at Woolwich until 1741. Another innovative move originating in Holland was the work written by the Dutch lawyer Edward Grotius, who in 1625 published his book entitled On the Law of War and Peace, which for the first time attempted to lay out a code of conduct for the military. The rules and regulations surrounding warfare were

The casting techniques of gun founders at this period had greatly improved, as is illustrated by these bronze-barrelled cannon. They show how guns of uniformity were being produced to standardize ammunition and the training of gunners.

therefore now being formalized, and the military establishments educated in the ways of how wars should be fought.

In the seventeenth century the process of the blast furnace was developed, and this signified a revolution in the way iron was smelted. The introduction of this technique had far-reaching implications regarding the way iron was produced and smelted; first and foremost it allowed an increase in the production of barrels for artillery. The blast furnace functions by removing unwanted impurities when a blast of air is forced through a mixture of solid fuel and ore to burn off the impurities; these are then removed as insoluble 'slag'. As refinement processes improved, the foundry techniques spread, leading to more countries becoming less dependent on the great gun foundries established in the sixteenth century. These emergent countries, such as Sweden and Portugal, were also beginning to exploit their great mineral deposits, including copper, iron and tin. The gun founders themselves were now moving to areas where they could command better terms of employment and pay for their experience, and could also obtain security for their dependants.

The output of iron multiplied ten-fold at this time as miners tried to keep up with demand from the foundries. Copper and tin, essential to the production of the alloy brass, was also mined in greater quantities in order to meet demand for the brass guns required for naval artillery and the newer designs of guns for land

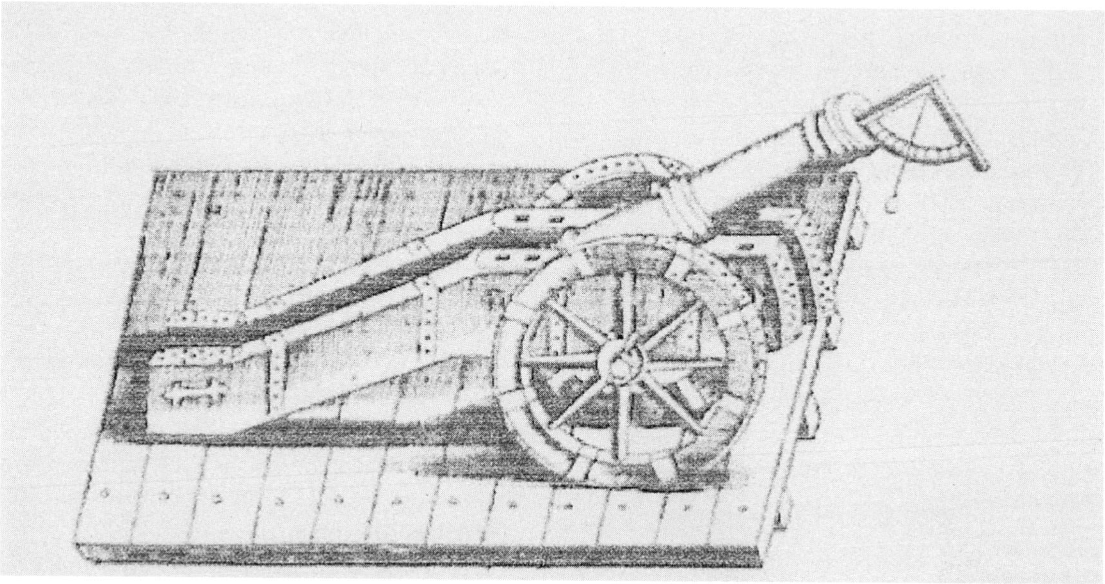

A cannon mounted on a wooden platform in order to spread the weight and thus prevent it from sinking into soft ground. The barrel is being elevated by means of a gunner's quadrant in order to aid the range towards the target.

service. Coal miners and charcoal burners, too, had to increase their output in order to fuel the furnaces. In fact it could be claimed that this was the first industrial revolution.

As the seventeenth century progressed, a range of tactical developments influenced the style of gunnery, leading to a more scientific approach in the use of the guns. Master gunners were beginning to look at how best to deploy their artillery in order that they might support other branches of the army during particular phases of a battle. They could still only fire by 'line of sight', which means that a target could only be engaged if it was in view. If there was a natural obstacle such as woodland or a hill screening the target, then the gunners could not fire at it. Projectiles with an average weight of between 5lb and 60lb (2.2 and 27kg) were by this time being fired out to ranges in excess of 2,000yd (1,800m), far greater than those engagement distances encountered during naval battles.

The main type of ammunition being used at this time was still solid shot, but hollow cast shells, referred to as either shells or bombs, were being filled with gunpowder and fused to explode in the air or on landing. These were usually fired during sieges against fortifications, where their high angle of trajectory propelled them over the walls.

SCANDINAVIA

This whole period was punctuated by many dozens of wars and hundreds of battles, each caused by a unique set of circumstances. Wars of territory were very common, such as the Spanish-Portuguese wars, in which countries used their armies, invariably supported by their artillery force, in order to establish independence or to make territorial gains. One such incident is recorded during the War of Kalmar, which broke out in 1611 and led to fighting between Sweden and Denmark, allied to Norway. The war lasted until 1613, the root cause being attributable to Sweden, ruled by King Charles IX, that was attempting to gain control of the region known as Finnmark in northern Norway.

In May 1612, at Elfsbourg in Sweden, the town and castle were besieged in a relatively minor operation by a combined force of Danish and English troops. At this engagement it is recorded that:

> Parts of the English forces came before Elsborough Castell in Sweden on Thurdaye the 14 of Maye and landed on Satterdaye the 16 of the said month. Then was the ordnance planted, and on Frydaye the 22th by 7 a clocke in the morning the King began to playe with 7 peeces upon one of the towers of the castell contynually tyll ten a clocke, at which tyme he had beaten downe parte of the tower, having spent 200 shot. ... at 2 a clocke the same daye... he commaunded the cannon to playe agayn, and before 5 a clocke (having drawne downe more greate peeces) he had with 286 shott made a breache for 3 to enter abrest.

The siege had lasted several days, which in warfare is seen as being a brief affair; but it had shown how well the English artillery could conduct itself in battle.

This involvement by England in a totally foreign war was just the first of such forays into overseas affairs. King James I of England had given his support to King Christian IV of Denmark, who had dispatched an expeditionary force to the mouth of the Gota and Kalmar, an area to which they laid siege and finally occupied. The war was resolved in January 1613 at the Peace of Knarod, which was brought about as a result of mediation by James I of England. Sovereignty of Finnmark was awarded to Denmark and Norway, and the territorial dispute was declared at an end. The war had not gone in Sweden's favour, and the country's troubles had been compounded when King Charles IX had died during the summer of 1611. In October that year the crown of Sweden was passed to the late king's son, the young prince Gustavus Adolphus. Aged only sixteen years old at the time when such great responsibility was thrust on him, Gustavus Adolphus, despite his youth, distinguished himself in battle during the remaining period of the Kalmar War.

GUSTAVUS ADOLPHUS

Gustavus Adolphus ruled Sweden from 1611 until his death in 1632, during which time he established himself as one of the most influential military figures of the period. From the very beginning of his reign Gustavus was an astute statesman, and even though he was royalty, he was deeply interested in his army and the artillery force in particular; in fact he valued his artillery so highly that he established a special school for the education of his artillerymen's children. He realized that artillerymen should be professional soldiers, and in return for relinquishing their civilian status, a contract was drawn up to reward them for their decision. Thus an artilleryman enjoyed the following benefits: his monthly wage would be doubled for every fortress captured or siege broken; he could not be court-martialled by a provost marshal; his wife and children could travel with him; he had the right

Illustration showing King Gustavus Adolphus of Sweden on campaign in the early seventeenth century. The artist depicts infantry deployment, and cavalry and artillery using tactics of the time.

not to stand in line for his food; and finally, he did not have to plunder, because he had the automatic right to claim all church bells from a captured town or city and these could be sold to the king for melting into artillery weapons. In return, gunners had to be loyal, steadfast and exceptionally accurate.

Like his French counterpart King Henry IV, Gustavus made truly astonishing changes to the way in which the Swedish army used its artillery, and to its construction. These changes were implemented by Lennart Torstensson, who at the tender age of twenty-seven was considered by many to be the best artilleryman of the period; the way in which he reorganized the Swedish artillery had a direct influence on the way in which the armies of other countries viewed their artillery force and its tactical use on the battlefield. One of his first moves was to organize the Swedish artillery force into a cohesive and permanent establishment comprising six companies. From these he created four companies of gunners and one of sappers, and a special unit equipped with a 'special exploding device': this was no doubt a 'petardier' force, whose role it was to demolish stout doors and walls with a device called a 'petard'. This item was often bell-shaped, and concentrated the force of the blast towards one area in order to maximize damage. It was a dangerous practice but virtually guaranteed to produce results, and soon petardier forces were to be found in armies all across Europe.

Gustavus worked very closely with Torstensson, and it is because of his personal involvement with artillery development at this time that he has been afforded the title 'The father of modern field artillery'. Furthermore his bravery in battle earned him another title, that of 'Lion of the North'. It is not known whether the concept of using massed mobile artillery fire on the battlefield was devised by Gustavus on his own, or working together with Torstensson. The planned changes were clearly motivated because Gustavus hated the fact that much of the artillery's potential heavy firepower was being wasted. He realized that existing tactics prevented the artillery from providing fire support to the infantry and cavalry as they manoeuvred on the battlefield, so he devoted much of his time trying to bring about a workable solution to this problem.

One of the first moves he made was to reduce the weight of artillery pieces. Through a series of firing trials it was discovered that it was possible to shorten the length of the barrel and to reduce its thickness; this decreased the overall amount of metal in the barrel, which made the weapon lighter. The next move was to improve and standardize the gunpowder used by Swedish artillery. A mixture was produced that burned at a uniform rate, thereby negating any problems to accuracy due to the shortened barrel, and also restoring any ballistic power which may have been lost by lightening the tube. Every stage in these transformations was overseen by Gustavus himself, so he was fully aware of developments.

THE LEATHER GUNS

It could be said that Gustavus was following the example set by Maurice of Nassau from the sixteenth century, when he standardized his artillery force around three set calibres: twenty-four-pounder, twelve-pounder and six-pounder guns. A long series of experiments under the king's personal supervision led to the full production of a fourth piece, the so-called 'regiment piece'. This was a light but sturdy three-pounder regimental gun, so light that only two horses were required to move it; moreover in an emergency the weapon could be pulled by one horse, or if necessary it could be handled by two or three men. The ball was directly secured to a bagged charge of gunpowder, called a cartridge, which gave unprecedented rapidity of fire due to the fact that it was loaded as a single round of ammunition rather than two separate items.

These regiment pieces, sometimes referred to as battalion guns, were produced as high priority weapons. They were to be the secret weapon in Gustavus' arsenal, known either as 'leather guns' or 'Kalter' guns. Some sources claim that these new guns were in service by 1621, when Sweden was at war with Poland. However, it is known that at that date the new guns were not yet common knowledge, and had not been shown to the Swedish king.

At the time of Sweden's military reorganization a number of foreign military planners were being attracted to the country, no doubt seeking financial reward for their expertise. One such man was Melchior Wurmbrandt, a colonel in the Austrian army to whom is credited the fact that he showed the design of the new and revolutionary lightweight piece of artillery to the Swedes in about 1625. Wurmbrandt's design, which was to become the famous 'leather gun', may have been based in turn on a similar design the colonel had seen in Zurich, Switzerland, in about 1622.

On seeing the plans of this weapon, Gustavus obviously realized the benefits it could bring, and was so impressed that he placed an order with Wurmbrandt for the production of such guns, capable of firing projectiles weighing 3lb and 6lb (1.4 and 2.7kg). In the event, it was the three-pounder gun that he came to favour, and he subsequently ordered that each regiment of foot and horse in his army should be equipped with one of these weapons. Later this level of equipping would rise to two guns for each regiment, and so it was that the three-pounder 'leather gun' became the more widely used and famous.

But the full credit of developing the leather gun does not belong to Wurmbrandt alone.

Some sources tell of a Scottish mercenary who took the idea to Sweden from Scotland, where it is claimed the weapon was invented. The other person who deserves credit in the development of the leather was an Englishman by the name of Robert Scott. He is known to have been involved with the weapon, and for his services Gustavus appointed him to the rank of quartermaster general. This fact is borne out by the epitaph on Robert Scott's headstone in Lambeth Church in London, which reads: 'Invented the leather ordnance and carried to the Kinge of Sweden 200 men, who, after ten years service for his worth and valour was preferred to the office of Quarter Mr. General of His Matie Army.' This makes for a very compelling case, and does complete the story of the gun's development and introduction into service.

There were various types of leather gun, and some sources claim that Wurmbrandt and Scott developed two separate versions of the weapon. Generally speaking, all were made with a thinly cast, iron outer barrel, into which was fitted a lining of copper capable of firing a projectile weighing 24oz (680g) with a calibre of little more than 2in (5cm). The barrel was supported by longitudinal iron bars attached to metal braces. A binding of rope and three wooden rings were fitted over the barrel, and shrunk on to this was a covering of leather. The barrel of the standard leather gun was just less than 6ft 6in (2m) in length and looked like a conventional cast barrel.

It is claimed that Wurmbrandt's barrel design weighed only 90lb (40kg), and that Scott's barrel was even lighter, at 45lb (20kg). It was long believed by some sources that the leather and rope provided reinforcement measures, but such coverings were more probably intended to prevent the onset of corrosion. The whole weapon on its carriage, and ready for battle, weighed just over 620lb (280kg). But there was a price to pay: due to their lightweight construction the guns did not have a long service life and were constantly having to be replaced. It was this failing that eventually led to it being taken out of service, and replaced by conventional weapons with a cast barrel. In the meantime, the enemies of Sweden came to envy and fear these small but powerful weapons.

THE THIRTY YEARS WAR

In 1618, only five years after being crowned king of Sweden, Gustavus Adolphus found himself thrust into another war. It began as a religious conflict between the Roman Catholics and Protestants of the Prussian States, but eventually involved several European countries, including England, and became a political war. It continued until 1648, going through a number of distinct phases, and became known to historians as the 'Thirty Years War'.

The first phase of the war was known as the 'Bohemian Period', and it was at this point that King James I involved England in what was an otherwise purely European conflict. It was the defeat of his son-in-law, Frederick, king of Bohemia, by Archduke Ferdinand, that brought about his intervention in 1620. It was decided that an army of 30,000 men should be sent to support his son-in-law, but the costs involved were enormous. It was estimated that £2,000,000 would be required to raise and equip such a force, and a further £900,000 per year to maintain the army in the field. In the end James elected for a drastically scaled-down token force, and 2,000 volunteers joined the war. Later, volunteer forces would mobilize for service in Europe, such as

A recreated field piece from the seventeenth century. The construction of the carriage is simple yet very strong, able to withstand movement over long distances, and the strain of being fired and moved on the battlefield.

the 6,000 men who went to fight in Holland in 1624. In 1625 an ill-fated force of 12,000 more men went to Germany; by the end of that year only 1,200 of these were still alive. One observer wrote: 'Such a rabble of raw and poor rascals have not been lightly seen, and they go so unwillingly that they must rather be driven than led.' But from this would emerge an officer cadre with valuable experience in warfare, which would stand them in good stead when they chose to join their elected sides during the English Civil War in 1642.

At the time of the outbreak of the Thirty Years War Sweden had no 'leather guns' in service, but nine years later at the siege of Wormditt in October 1627 there were enough of these weapons in service to make their presence felt. Obviously these new guns were too light for siege operations, but they showed how they could be moved quickly and easily over ground for redeployment elsewhere to provide fire support on the battlefield. By 1628, Gustavus' troops took at least eight of these guns with them to the mouth of the Vistula river, where they manhandled them over rough terrain to fire on a Polish fleet and inflict severe damage. An English account of the Swedish leather guns dating from August 1628 states that they were:

> …as good and better service than his Copper Cannon: for as fast as the souldiers are able to march, the Cannon is convayed along with them, having but one horse to draw but the

> biggest of them, and three or foure men can carry the biggest of them on their shoulders over any straight place, or narrow Bridge whatsoever, so that the Polls are not aware ere the Cannon play upon them, for it will shoot as great force as any other: which make the Palonians say, his Maiestie useth Devilrie: but that is all untrue: for I my selfe have heard those Cannon severall times shot with as great force as any other.

This indicates that the high standard of training was paying dividends, and that the Swedish gunners could be so audacious in their tactics that it completely caught their enemy off guard. In 1629 at the Battle of Honigfeld the Swedes suffered a great loss when ten of their secret leather guns were captured by Polish forces. As with all such secret weapons, when captured it wasn't long before their details were made universal knowledge and each army could develop its own form of regimental gun.

During the course of the Thirty Years War the armies of France, Spain, Holland, Denmark, the various Prussian States and Austria all fought across the continent. Countries were ravaged and war-torn, and none more so than some Prussian states. All the while the armies were gaining valuable lessons in warfare, especially the artillery; in fact, one could consider this war as being a training and proving ground for future officers and weapon development. The Austrian artillery force, for example, was trained not to waste ammunition, and was encouraged to hit the target by the fourth shot. One unattributable account concerns an Austrian army officer regaling a battery of artillery and threatening them with hanging if they did not hit the target. Generally speaking, Austrian gunners ranged with three trial shots, after which they could concentrate on the targets. The accuracy of Austrian gunners became legendary. One account tells how an Austrian battery shot the 'ears' off a town's alarm bell, and thereby prevented the news of the attack being rung. On another occasion an Austrian gunner is reputed to have cut the anchor chain of an enemy warship and left it to drift helplessly on the tide.

2 The Years 1626–1650

PORTUGAL

One nascent state at this time was Portugal, and its increasing influence was to have a lasting effect on operations both at sea and on land. It had important trading links in the East Indies and South America, and this would bring it into conflict with other European states. In the first half of the century it was closely linked to Spain, but it was not an amicable relationship, and Spain treated Portugal more like a province, thereby causing great unrest. Portugal mounted two revolts against Spain, the first in 1633 and the second in 1637, but despite French support these actions collapsed. In 1640 Portugal was more successful and finally gained its independence from Spain, and John Duke of Braganza was elected as King John IV. But even before these events, Portugal was strengthening the overseas empire that it had started to carve out for itself. In 1630, the Portuguese ejected the Dutch from Brazil, as some sort of recompense for losing trade routes in the Far East to the Dutch and English. The wars with Spain weakened Portugal, but the fighting reaffirmed it as an independent state.

Portuguese gun founders had long been active, and it was a practice they maintained. In 1627 they were casting pieces of artillery up to 8.7in (22cm) calibre, which placed the weapon in the category of cannon royal and comparable to anything being cast in other European states at that time. The country was beginning to exploit its mineral resources such as iron, tin and copper, all of which could be used in the manufacture of artillery. In fact, with tin and copper at their disposal, Portuguese gun founders were able to cast bronze cannon barrels and establish indigenous centres of weapons production, which meant the country was less dependent on overseas states for the importing of weapons.

The seventeenth century would see a degree of ascendancy in Portuguese military fortunes. For example, in May 1644, a Portuguese force of between 7,000 and 8,000 troops, commanded by Matias Alberquerque, mounted a campaign into neighbouring Spain. The army included 1,600 cavalry and was supported by only six pieces of artillery. The campaign culminated in the brief but serious Battle of Montijo on 26 May of that same year. The Spanish army, commanded by the Baron of Molingen, numbered 4,400; it included 1,700 cavalry and only four guns. The battle commenced with the usual opening exchange of artillery fire, which lasted about one hour, after which it developed into an action involving cavalry and infantry.

The Spanish adopted a very aggressive action, and pressed home their attacks with such vigour that the superior Portuguese forces were overwhelmed and began to collapse. Despite the fact that the Spanish were outnumbered, they continued to attack with great ferocity, which compelled Alberquerque to adopt a fighting withdrawal. He retreated in such good order that his army was able to take their artillery with them. The Spanish had lost 433 killed and 375 wounded, but lacked the money to pursue an offensive against Portugal, and they could ill afford the troops. The Portuguese lost about 4,000 men, and although the action had been relatively minor in terms of artillery involvement, it did secure the borders between the two countries in favour of Portugal. During the short campaign the Portuguese army had been supported by French and Dutch mercenaries, and although England was by that time engaged in a fierce civil war, troops were sent to support the action (it is not clear whether these were Royalist or Parliamentarian).

THE THIRTY YEARS WAR CONTINUED

The Thirty Years War had a serious impact right across Europe; it also led to the emergence of more professional armies. Although there were many leading statesmen at the time, it was Gustavus Adolphus who stood out above all the rest. Gustavus realized that the war would be completely different from any that had been fought previously: in a letter to his chancellor, Axel Oxenstierna, he wrote: 'All the wars that are on foot in Europe have been fused together, and become a single war.'

He was, of course, correct in this assessment, but what he could not have known was that the war would continue to be fought through various phases until 1648. Eventually, field commanders and state rulers between them came to realize that after several years of fighting, the Thirty Years War was no longer simply about religion, and were astute enough to realize that it was now a struggle of politics and territorial gains. At the time of the war it has been estimated that the combined population of Sweden and Denmark was 1.5 million, whilst that of the Holy Roman Empire, with its mainly Catholic population, was in the order of twelve million. Despite this disparity, the Swedish army led by Gustavus proved to be more than a match for the larger armies. This was mainly due to the way in which the Swedish artillery force was handled on the battlefield and the enigmatic commanders within Gustavus' army.

The phase of the Thirty Years War known as the 'Swedish Period' began in July 1630 when Gustavus advanced into the areas of Stettin and Mecklenburg, northern states of Prussia within the Holy Roman Empire. It lasted until 1634, and culminated at the disastrous Battle of Nordlingen in September that year. The Swedish army had numbered 30,000 when it landed at Usedom on the Baltic coast, but quickly expanded to 40,000 men as it marched inland. These new recruits to the ranks of Gustavus' army came from Prussian states such as Saxony, and they fought alongside him at major engagements. Included in this force were at least eighty of the famous leather guns, with many more available, along with siege artillery, which could be quickly brought up by the re-supply column as it followed in the wake of the army. The mobile leather guns were light enough to be moved anywhere very quickly on the battlefield where they could be deployed to support musketeers.

Before Gustavus' reformation the ratio of artillery to infantry in the Swedish army had been 2.5 guns per one thousand troops. By 1630 this had been increased to 9.4 guns per thousand men, giving his force a huge advantage in firepower. This was a much better proportion than any other European army, including some Prussian states that at the time deployed only one gun per thousand men. At the Battle of Breitenfeld 17 September 1631, the first major battle since Sweden had landed fourteen months previously, each of the infantry squadrons of Gustavus' army was equipped with two or three of the 'regimental' leather guns. Through the judicious use of clergy and local juries, Gustavus had been to recruit a reinforcement army of 40,000. These new troops were '...strong of limb, and, so far as can be ascertained, courageous – in years from eighteen to thirty'. Another historian of the period noted of the Swedish army that it had '...firm discipline, high courage and mobile cannon'. It was this combination of fire from infantry weapons and canister shot being fired by the Swedish artillery that devastated the enemy on the battlefield.

Back in Sweden, those men employed in the manufacture of armaments such as artillery and other munitions and transport were considered to be in 'reserved occupations', and as such were exempt from military service. This made complete sense because an experienced workforce would produce a supply of reliable weaponry essential to the functioning of the army on campaign. Sweden was still in the ascendancy stage in terms of military capability on the battlefield, and also materially in the form of weaponry. Like England and Portugal, the country had rich mineral deposits including iron and copper that the country was able to use to its advantage. In addition there were coal deposits, forests for charcoal, and many waterways, all essential for providing fuel and energy to power the foundries producing weapons. Indeed, the Royal Swedish Household actively encouraged the development of the country's armaments industry, because as well as supplying its own needs for iron and bronze guns, the country could also then export more and more. For example, in the space of twenty years, between 1626 and 1646, the weight of cast-iron guns exported by Sweden rose from only twenty-two tons per year to more than 1,000 tons.

Blocks of pikemen would often be deployed during seventeenth-century battles in order to protect the artillery from cavalry charges. The pikes could be as long as 18ft (5.5m) in length, and sufficient to disrupt all but the most determined attack.

THE BATTLE OF BREITENFELD

The Battle of Breitenfeld on 17 September 1631 was the first major engagement following fourteen months of siege warfare at cities

A recreated scene showing the tactics of seventeenth-century warfare. The artillery has suspended firing as the forces close with one another in front of the gun positions.

such as Magdeburg, and otherwise general manoeuvring. Gustavus commanded an army of 40,000 men, supported by an artillery force of between sixty and seventy guns, mainly of the regimental 'leather' type. Facing him across the battlefield was Count Johan Tilly, commanding an army of 32,000 men with an artillery force of thirty guns. These weapons were not very mobile, being twenty-four-pounders, each of which required twenty horses to move them. Furthermore, each of Tilly's supply wagons supporting the artillery force required twelve horses to pull each one. There was little chance that such heavy and cumbersome weapons could be moved during battle, even in the best of conditions. Tilly was aged sixty years and had gained much experience in warfare and was known to favour Spanish tactics on the battlefield.

Tilly had been involved in the fighting battles during the Thirty since 1626, during the Bohemian period. He was persuaded by his impetuous lieutenant, Count Gottfried zu Pappenheim, to take up battle positions at Breitenfeld, four miles north of Leipzig. In fact, it was the intention to recover Leipzig from the Imperialist-Catholic pact that led to this particular engagement. Pappenheim commanded the cavalry on the left flank of the army, while Tilly commanded the infantry on the right flank. The army took up positions, forming themselves into tercios, a Spanish tactic of forming squares containing 1,500 to 2,000 men. A total of seventeen such formations formed line abreast with the artillery placed in two groups on the right wing of the army and facing the Saxons force in Gustavus' army.

At the time of the battle Gustavus was aged thirty-seven; his Master Gunner, Lennart Torstensson, was barely thirty-two. They were energetic and innovative commanders, who left behind them a legacy that had far-reaching implications for armies of the future. Despite his young age, compared to more experienced and senior commanders, Torstensson proved to be an eager exponent of artillery, which, along with his willingness to learn, had led to his being recognized as a Master Gunner. The Swedish army took up positions formed into either half or full brigades in order that his musketeers might be protected by the pikemen and able to deliver their fire in volleys.

The two forces had been encamped opposite one another overnight, but when the Swedish army began to move into position on the morning of 17 September the historian C.R.L. Fletcher described the movement thus: 'Each brigade was like a little movable fortress with its curtains and ravelins, and each part would be able to come to the assistance of the other.' The Swedish army took up twenty-nine separate positions, not counting the Saxon force, each commanded by a capable officer. The cavalry was placed on the flanks, and regimental guns, each served by two men, were deployed with each brigade. The heavy artillery was placed directly in front of the centre, under the command of Torstensson, facing Tilly's artillery. This formation gave the Swedish army depth and breadth to their positions, while the enemy had only a broad frontage to their positions.

The battle opened at noon with an exchange of artillery fire. Colonel Robert Monro, commanding an infantry unit in the centre of the Swedish army, wrote of the effects of the artillery barrage:

> With Trumpets sounding, Drummes beating, and Colours advanced and flying… the enemy was thundering amongst us, with the noise and roaring whistle of Cannon-Bullets; where you may imagine the hurt was great; the sound of such musick being scarce worth hearing… then our cannon begun to roare, great and small, paying the enemy with the like coyne, which thundering continued alike on both sides for two hours and a half, during which time, our Battailes of horse and foot stood firme like a wall, the Cannon now and then making great breaches amongst us, which was diligently looked into…'

The imperial cavalry attempted to take the Swedish right flank, but were prevented from doing so by the simple expedient of extending the flank under attack. The fighting ebbed backwards and forwards for nearly three hours, during which time there was much exchange of musket and artillery fire. But Gustavus' gunners were so well trained, and because they were using the fixed type of ammunition of the iron projectile fitted to the bagged charge, they were able to fire three times for every shot fired by Tilly's gunners. At extreme close range artillery was taking a toll, and Torstensson directed his guns to fire directly into the massed infantry squares. The Swedish troops, confident in the knowledge that they had superior artillery firepower, went completely on to the offensive, with Gustavus leading a charge against the left of Tilly's line.

The outcome of the battle meant that German Protestantism was assured, and that Sweden had emerged as a major military power. Breitenfeld showed how cavalry could be thrown back by the firepower of artillery. The Swedish artillery had shown a masterful combination of flexibility and mobility, elements that would become the hallmark of Gustavus' artillery. Count Tilly was severely wounded in the action and withdrew, having lost 7,000 men killed and 6,000 taken prisoner. The Swedes had suffered 2,100 killed and wounded, and their Saxon allies had lost about 4,000 men. Colonel Monro wrote that the Saxon losses '…did not exceed three thousand men, most killed by the enemies Cannons'.

In addition to the regimental guns sited in depth and breadth with their attachments, the

Swedes maintained a small reserve force in the rear. These could be brought forward at a moment's notice to replace losses among the units, or to lend fire support during the final attack. These regimental guns were extremely flexible, and the men serving them were so well trained they could fire them at an extraordinary speed: by using shot fixed to the bagged charge they could load and fire eight times for every six shots fired by musketeers.

Another innovation introduced into the arsenal of the Swedish artillery was a new type of ammunition called 'grape shot'. This was a multiple projectile anti-personnel munition, designed to be totally devastating at close range. Grape shot was used for the sole purpose of halting, or at least breaking charges by infantry and cavalry. As with other developments, this new type of projectile underwent a series of changes and appeared in various forms: most common was the type comprising a wooden disc fitted with a central post, around which were mounted several iron balls about the size of a large egg; these were then covered with material such as canvas. This was secured by cord wound in such a way as to hold each ball in place, producing a munition that looked like a bunch of grapes; the term was soon adopted to identify it. Grape shot was loaded in exactly the same way as a single cast-iron ball projectile or canister shot, the other anti-personnel munition. On being fired, the wooden disc shattered and the canvas covering burnt away, allowing the several projectiles to spread over an area in front of the gun's position.

A variation on the canvas-covered balls was a version with three layers of balls, separated by wooden discs. The effect of several guns firing grape shot simultaneously against infantry or cavalry advancing across the open would have been truly deadly.

THE BATTLE OF LUTZEN

Gustavus made the most of his success at Breitenfeld, and by the end of 1631 he was in control of most of the northern states within the Holy Roman Empire. He had an army of at least 80,000, and Emperor Ferdinand was extremely concerned. In April 1632 Ferdinand recalled the forty-nine-year-old Count Albrecht von Wallenstein as commander of his forces. Never popular with his own troops or commanders, he had entered the career of soldiering rather late in life. He had seen military action during earlier campaigns in the Thirty Years War, and enjoyed success against the Danes in 1627, but he had been dismissed in August 1630 by Emperor Ferdinand following pressure by other commanders. Wallenstein's presence brought about a change in operations, and the imperial forces began to fight back against the seemingly unstoppable Swedish army.

By mid-April Gustavus had crossed the River Danube and entered Bavaria, where he advanced towards positions held by Count Johan Tilly and Maximilian of Bavaria. The two sides met at the River Lech on 15–16 April, and the Swedish army immediately mounted an aggressive attack. Count Tilly was mortally wounded in the fighting and his retreating army left behind most of its artillery, which had been abandoned along with the baggage train. The Swedes now had control of Augsberg, Munich and southern Bavaria. Gustavus with 20,000 men decided to march towards Nuremberg, but he was being followed by Wallenstein who had joined forces with Maximilian of Bavaria: together they had a much larger army of 60,000 men. The Swedish army entered Nuremberg, whilst Wallenstein occupied positions near Furth and the Castle of Alte Veste, where he ordered trenches to be dug. For weeks the armies faced one another, the campaign falling into stalemate. The historian Gindley wrote that '...all Europe waited with anxiety and hope for news'.

By the end of July and into August, supplies were beginning to run short, and Gustavus took the opportunity to send for reinforcements. These fresh troops arrived around mid-August and brought his strength up to 45,000. Supplies were still very short, and sickness was beginning to break out in the encampments due to their limited sanitary conditions. On 4 September Gustavus decided to attack Alte Veste, which was by this time heavily entrenched by Wallenstein. But the ground across which the Swedes had to advance was not suited to cavalry charges, and their vulnerable artillery could not be brought forward. The infantry, weakened by sickness and without support, were thrown back, with at least 3,000 killed. Gustavus was losing more men through sickness, and on 18 September he withdrew towards Vienna. The Swedish army, which many had thought to be invincible, had suffered its first defeat.

Wallenstein wasted no time and marched towards Saxony. Gustavus responded to this move and marched northwards, crossing the River Saale with a force of 20,000 men. Between 9 and 15 November the Swedish army entrenched itself at Naumberg as it awaited reinforcements and re-supply. Wallenstein by now had joined with Count Pappenheim, whom he directed towards the town of Halle; he himself took up entrenched positions around Lutzen. On learning of these moves Gustavus decided to march out from his camp at the Kosen defile at Naumburg, and, despite being numerically weak, to attack at Lutzen.

The opening gambits leading up to the Battle of Lutzen began on the evening of 15 November when Gustavus set out towards Pegau to link up with his Saxon allies. By 5am he had not made contact with them, and he moved towards Wallenstein, whom he was determined to destroy in battle. The Swedish king stated that the '...die was now cast', and that he could not bear to have him under his beard '...and not make a swoop on him'. For his part Wallenstein was alerted to the approach of Gustavus, and made ready his positions and his troops: '...spent that whole night in digging and intrenching, in embattling the army and planting the artillery'.

King Gustavus Adolphus, 1611–32, killed at the Battle of Lutzen in 1632. He is credited with the introduction of light field guns and cartridges, and was the first tactician to class his artillery into categories. He also introduced massed formations of artillery to overwhelm the enemy forces with weight of firepower.

At around 2am on the morning of 16 November 1632, Wallenstein was informed that Gustavus was barely one mile from his position. An urgent dispatch was sent to Pappenheim: 'Sir, let everything else be, and hurry with all your forces and artillery back to me.' The plain at Lutzen across which the battle would be fought was flat and low-lying, and the two armies drew up their positions to face one another across the Liepzig Road, a raised route that bisects the area running south-west to north-east. Wallenstein had 25,000 men at his immediate disposal, along with sixty or sixty-six gun; when Pappenheim arrived he would have 8,000 reinforcements. The Swedish army comprised 19,000 troops, supported by twenty-six heavy guns and at least forty regimental guns.

A thick fog enveloped the battlefield until 11am, when it began to clear: immediately the Swedish artillery opened fire. According to the historian Fleetwood, who watched the battle: 'the cannons played a while, but we were presently under ffavour of their canons'. The armies were arranged in a broad front, but the Swedish army had depth. Wallenstein's guns were sited at two positions: the first was on his right flank, taking advantage of the height provided by the Wind Mill Hill; the second faced Gustavus' heavy guns, slightly to the right of his centre.

The Swedish army began the battle by attacking the enemy's right flank in a charge led by Gustavus; this forced the infantry back from their positions, and a cavalry charge led by Heinrich Holk was driven back on to their own artillery. Wallenstein countered by launching a concerted cavalry charge, which threatened the Swedish centre. Then the fog that had earlier hampered operations descended once more across the battlefield and caused great confusion. Gustavus was riding to the threatened position in an attempt to rally his troops when he became separated from the regiment of cavalry he was leading. In the company of two or three other riders he was temporarily disorientated and was suddenly confronted by a unit of enemy cavalry: in the

A recreated scene depicting how warfare in the seventeenth century was conducted. The artillery could only fire against the enemy in the open, and when the opposing sides closed with one another they would not risk firing for fear of killing their own troops.

mêlée Gustavus was mortally shot in the head and body. As news of his death spread across the battlefield, Bernard of Saxe-Weimar, who had been commanding the Swedish left flank, took charge of the battle.

At this point Pappenheim arrived on the battlefield and launched an attack that forced the Swedes to withdraw back across the Leipzig Road. This action did nothing to influence the outcome, and Pappenheim was killed in the fighting. Sensing victory to be in their grasp, despite the loss of their king, the Swedes fought on with their cavalry, driving off the remnants of Wallenstein's army and seizing their artillery. The imperialist forces had lost 12,000 men, and the Swedes about 10,000. It remained one of the most sanguinary battles of the entire war, but it did reaffirm Swedish artillery and battlefield tactics as instilled into the army by Gustavus: even though his inspired leadership was lost, the legacy of his innovative approach to artillery remained.

The Swedish army campaigned for a further two years under the leadership of commanders such as Bernard of Saxe-Weimar and General Gustavus Horn. But the true spirit and tactical genius had really gone from the army, a change that became evident only two years after the death of Gustavus when the Swedish army fought the Battle of Nordlingen, on 6 September 1634. At this engagement they faced a Spanish army of 20,000 led by Prince Ferdinand, who was supported by his cousin, also called Ferdinand, leading an army of 35,000. The Swedish army of 16,000 foot and 9,000 horse was led by Horn and Bernard, both capable commanders who should have realized the situation and refused battle. Despite the unfavourable odds, the Swedish army still fought fiercely, but at a cost of 12,000 killed and 6,000 taken prisoner. The Catholic forces of the two Ferdinands suffered 2,000 casualties. Equally crushing was the fact that some eighty valuable pieces of Swedish artillery had been captured.

This engagement marked the end of Sweden's direct involvement in the Thirty Years War. However, some Swedish troops still served on, such as Lennart Torstensson, who had served the Swedish artillery so well under Gustavus Adolphus; at the Battle of Jankau on 6 March 1645 he produced a sterling victory, and this brought about a favourable treaty between Saxony and Sweden.

Battles of the Thirty Years War continued until the Peace of Westphalia was declared on 24 October1648; this finally brought an end to the fighting. The Holy Roman Empire and France signed the Treaty of Munster, and Sweden signed the Treaty of Osnabruck. The war had devastated communities, with some eight million people killed in addition to the 350,000 killed on the battlefield. In Bohemia, to the south of Prague, 29,000 villages and their communities were destroyed, and the story was repeated right across Prussia, in states such as Thuringia where only 627 houses remained. Livelihoods had been wiped out, trade halted and, to compound matters, bubonic plague, or the 'Black Death', added to the misery.

At the time of these occurrences King Charles I and his parliament were engaged in fighting the English Civil War, which brought its own form of hardships.

MORE TACTICAL CHANGES

Before Sweden's revolutionary changes, artillery had been consigned to a largely static function on the battlefield. When deploying for battle, artillery batteries were invariably

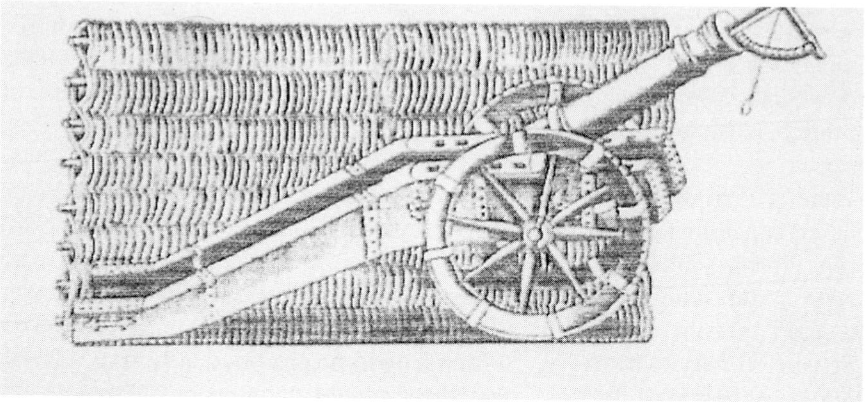

Cannon mounted on a wicker mat to prevent the weapon from sinking into soft earth on firing. This feature distributes the weight of the weapon and would make it easier to move after firing. The barrel is being elevated for range by means of a gunner's quadrant.

placed in the open field, and positioned well to the front of the battle order; like this they could be used to fire on the opposing side before the movement of battle closed in front of the guns' positions, thus prohibiting their use for fear of firing on their own troops. But in this location it stood the risk of being overrun by the enemy, as had happened at battles such as Breitenfeld and Lutzen.

Among the many lessons learned during the Thirty Years War was the fact that artillery had to be protected, especially during siege warfare. The defending garrison of a city under siege had the advantage that they could seek refuge behind the walls, and the artillerymen could load and fire their guns from the safety of the newly emerging military defences such as revelins or hornworks. The attacking artillerymen, on the other hand, were still exposed, and had to rely on fieldworks to provide them with protection, along with constructions called 'gabions': these were large wickerwork baskets filled with earth, their advantage being that they could be erected quickly.

The Thirty Years War had also shown that artillery fired from elevated positions could gain improved range, and it has been recorded in some of the books and pamphlets of the time that artillery '...was posted on an eminence, since a ball travels with greater force downhill than uphill'. Another benefit to positioning artillery on natural heights was that firepower could be brought to bear on a wide range of targets across the battlefield.

Initially the size and weight of guns meant that they were virtually immobile in battle, and until the advent of the Swedish leather gun, and other standardizations, it had always been accepted that artillery remained where it was sited for the duration of the battle. However, reducing the weight to make it easier to move was but one step forward in solving the problem. Another advantageous development was of a feature called a 'trail wheel'. Generally ascribed to Gustavus Adolphus, this device was simply a single wheel fitted on its own axle and equipped with a jointed handle. The trail of the carriage, which rested on the ground, was adapted to accept the insertion of this device. The gun was instantly made more freely mobile because of the articulated movement it permitted: for the first time a gun could be pulled breech end first. Before the appearance of the trail wheel, guns were generally pulled muzzle first, which was extremely awkward and labour-intensive.

3 The Years 1651–1675

RIFLING

As the seventeenth century progressed, further innovations were considered concerning the development of artillery; one of these was to provide rifling inside the barrels of the gun in order to improve accuracy. Rifling involves cutting a series of helical grooves into the interior of the barrel in order that they might impart spin to the projectile, thereby making it more stable during its trajectory towards the target. The idea of rifling had first been considered as early as the fourteenth century, but it was intended only for the muskets of the day. By 1600 King Christian IV of Denmark had equipped some of his troops with rifled muskets, and in 1680 French cavalry units were issued with weapons fitted with rifled barrels.

For artillery use the idea does not appear to have caught on, however, for a variety of reasons: first, after boring out the barrel, special reaming machines had to be used to cut the rifling grooves; this would have added an extra process to the manufacturing of barrels, with the result that output would have been reduced. Secondly, this extra machining of the barrel would have added considerably to the overall manufacturing cost. The third, and probably most important reason why rifling was not adopted for use in artillery at this point in history, is simply that it slowed down the time taken to reload the guns.

Projectiles loaded into a barrel equipped with rifling had to be physically forced down the barrel against the grooves. With a small-calibre musket this was possible, but with a projectile weighing several pounds the task would have taken too long, which would have been counter-productive on the battlefield. Furthermore, the gunpowder in use at the time produced a lot of carbon, which would have led to a build-up of fouling between the grooves of the rifling, thereby hampering loading even further. Rifling in artillery was not considered a viable option until the nineteenth century.

SIEGE WARFARE

Siege warfare is generally regarded as a form of warfare more usually associated with the Middle Ages, involving an army surrounding a castle in order to induce the defending garrison to surrender. The method of siege warfare that emerged during the seventeenth century was not entirely original, but was in fact based on methods that had been proven to work during various siege operations, such as those conducted at the siege of Raglan Castle in Wales in 1646 during the English Civil War. The tactics called for the attackers to move systematically towards the target, allowing them to advance their artillery ever closer, through a series of entrenchments. The main aim of the move was to enable the attackers to bring their siege artillery close enough forward to a range where it could fire against the walls of the target without being subjected to unduly heavy retaliatory fire from the defenders. From their positions the attackers sought to create a breach in the defensive walls with their artillery, which would then also provide covering fire for the infantry as it made its assault into this breach. In some instances, mining operations to dig under the walls were sufficient to allow the infantry assault without having to wait for the heavy siege artillery to breach the walls. These subterranean workings were completed by units of engineers and pioneers who were attached to the artillery train, and tasked with constructing positions for their own guns and demolishing the enemy's defences.

Siege warfare was governed by a number of factors, and the speed at which the advancing trench network could be advanced towards the target could vary. In such operations, time was of the essence, and under ideal conditions a siege operation could last somewhere between six and eight weeks before the garrison surrendered. Raglan Castle was an exception to the rule, the garrison finally surrendering on 19 August, having been besieged since June. (*See* Chapter 7, The English Civil War.) On the other hand, in 1673 the Dutch fortress of Maastrict capitulated after a siege of only two weeks: the French besiegers prepared their positions on 17–18 June, and on 1 July the commander was invited to surrender. He very wisely accepted the terms, and saved the lives of his troops.

The day Maastrict surrendered the courtesies of war were observed, and unnecessary loss of life was avoided. It had always been the case that if a garrison refused to surrender, the lives of the garrison and all its non-combatants were forfeit and they were put to the sword. This convention had been carried over into the seventeenth century, even though the observation was medieval in outlook. Typically, if a wall had been undermined, or the artillery had created a breach in the defensive walls, the besiegers would call on the defending garrison to see reason and surrender. The act of surrender in itself might not have prevented the attackers from plundering, but it would have reduced the wholesale destruction of the town. An exception is the siege of Basing House during the English Civil War in October 1645. This fortified manor house situated just outside Basingstoke in Hampshire was besieged by a Parliamentarian force well equipped with artillery. The Royalist garrison put up a spirited defence of the house, but their bravery was for nothing when finally they surrendered: frustration, and the fact that many of the garrison were Catholic, led to them being put to the sword, and the remains of the house destroyed by explosive charges of gunpowder.

MARSHAL SEBASTIEN LE PRESTRE DE VAUBAN

One man came to epitomize siege warfare and military architecture during the seventeenth century more than any other: the name Sebastien Le Prestre de Vauban became indelibly linked to the construction of defensive fortifications, and the operations to reduce enemy defences when on campaign in the service of his country. Born in 1633 to a rather undistinguished, humble Burgundian family, Vauban joined the army in 1651, serving as a volunteer under the rebel Prince of Condé during the War of the Fronde. The five-year war was due to resentment against the power being accumulated first by Cardinal Richelieu and then, after 1643, by Cardinal

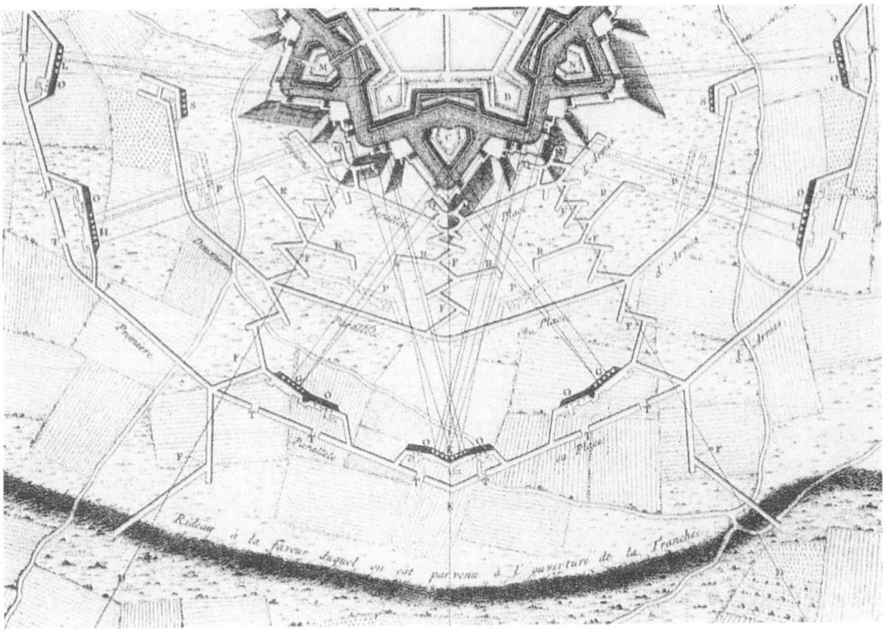

Advancing artillery towards the walls of a defended city. This method was devised and improved on by Sebastien le Prestre de Vauban.

Mazarin, who served King Louis XIV of France. It was a very much one-sided affair, and the Fronde collapsed in 1653 with Condé escaping to Spain. Vauban was taken prisoner, but he was more fortunate than many others because he was brought to the attention of Cardinal Mazarin who, possibly recognizing the man's potential military attributes, persuaded him to serve the royal household of France. It can't have been a difficult choice to make, especially when the alternative option would probably have been long-term imprisonment.

Following his change in allegiance, Vauban went on to serve an apprenticeship as an engineer under the Chavalier de Clerville, seeing service at the sieges of Clermont-en-Argonne and Sainte Menehoud. In 1655 he was appointed Engineer-in-Ordinary, and later on succeeded his master, de Clerville, as the Commissaire Générale des Fortifications in 1678, when he became known as 'the King's engineer'. He was hard-working, conscientious and energetic, qualities that led to him being promoted to the rank of lieutenant general in 1688, and later being created a Marshal of France.

Vauban's ideas on military thinking led to him dominating developments of the two diametrically opposed functions of siege warfare and fortification. Through him these two aspects of military thinking and planning would culminate in the ultimate capabilities for military forces limited by gunpowder weaponry then in current use. This was to prove extremely important in an age when siege warfare was still possible, but far from being one of the most common forms of military activity. Vauban was a forward-thinking man, and by drawing on those experiences and practices of the past one hundred years that were known to him through his studies, he was able to implement his ideas and consolidate them into practical solutions covering both fortification and siege warfare.

The method of siege warfare used by Vauban was not new, but by introducing his own theories he was able to bring the old practices up to date, and they would eventually go on to become standardized practice. The opportunity to prove these theories for the first time in battle came during the siege of Maastrict in 1673, a confrontation that was successfully concluded by using the new tactics. According to Vauban's principles, the first move in laying siege to a walled city was to construct a trench system that surrounded the target and lay just beyond the effective range of the defenders' artillery. Known as the 'first parallel', it was situated at about 1,000 yards (900m) from the walls of the city, and marked the beginning of the city's blockade. From this trench, engineers and pioneers would begin to dig a series of trenches leading towards the target from several selected points. These earthworks, known as 'saps', were constructed using a 'zigzag' method of approach, because this prevented the defenders from firing down the length of the trench and causing casualties. The spoil from the digging was heaped up to raise the level of the parapets for the added protection of the troops, who could then work uninterrupted and without being observed. The distance dug forward was usually fixed, because as the besiegers advanced they came within range of the defenders' artillery. The second parallel was then constructed about 300 yards (275m) away from the target.

The work was time-consuming and labour-intensive, but it produced results and kept casualties to a minimum. Using Vauban's instructions and working under his direction, a good sap might be pressed forwards at a rate of about 160 yards (146m) in twenty-four hours. When the second parallel was dug, additional earthworks were constructed at various points, and these served as emplacements for the batteries of siege artillery. Once the heavy guns had been moved forwards, they opened fire on the target from several directions. This put pressure on the defenders, who had to repair damage and attempt to return fire. As the range decreased, the defenders could return fire against the besiegers' gun positions with greater accuracy. In retaliation the attackers would fire great concentrations against the ramparts in an effort to force the defenders to take cover from the bombardments and reduce the effects of the defenders' artillery. With the city defences surrounded by artillery it was simply a question of time before a breach was made in the walls; once this was achieved the attacking infantry forces would assault forwards to enter the city.

There was always the possibility that the walls of the city might withstand the bombardment, in which case the engineers had to be prepared to dig further saps in the zigzag pattern and take their artillery closer to the walls. This work was completed under cover of fire from their own guns. Actually, the closer the works approached the walls, the less chance there was of being fired on directly by the defenders' guns, because they could not depress the barrels far enough. The attackers, on the other hand, could still fire at the elevated walls. The drawback to moving closer to the enemy was that it left the attackers vulnerable to the possibility that the defenders might rally and counterattack, thus forcing them to withdraw, abandoning the gun positions and the guns, even if only temporarily.

If the defenders did mount such an assault against the attackers there was the strong possibility that they might 'spike' the siege guns: this involved hammering nails or metal spikes into the touch holes or vents of the pieces of the guns, and doing so with such force that they could not be extracted. This meant that

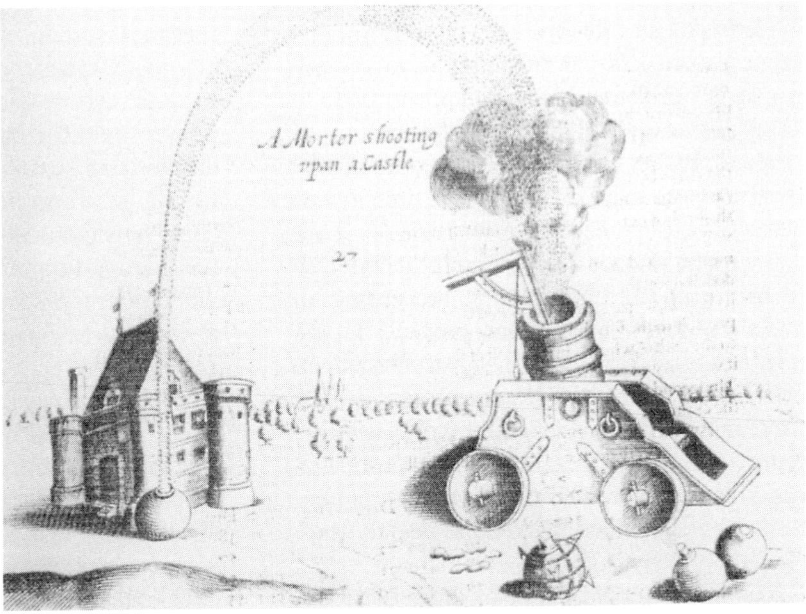

A seventeenth-century mortar being used against a defensive target. The range has been gauged using a gunner's quadrant. This particular type of weapon appears to be a variation of the mortar and is known as a trabuccho, from the fact that the trunnions are set well back to the breech end of the barrel.

the guns were rendered useless if they were recaptured by the besiegers in order to mount their own counter-attack, because with the touch holes blocked the guns could not be fired, and either replacement weapons had to be moved forward or the assault postponed. The attackers had to be ready for any eventuality, and strong forces of infantry were maintained constantly in the parallels to protect the guns and artillerymen against any attacks the defenders might launch.

Should the defensive walls remain undamaged and the garrison continue to resist, then the besiegers were left with no option but to construct a third parallel. The usual zigzag saps would be dug forwards, although at this close range they were vulnerable to harassing fire by musketeers; the range might now be as close as one hundred yards or less. Siege guns were usually effective at such close quarters, and battered the walls and gates to create a breach for the assaulting infantry. In the event of failure at this stage the attackers would bring forward their mortars in order to lob explosive bombs at high angles inside the defences. Vauban wrote his observations on the use of mortars at the site of a siege in 1672, where they were loaded: 'with up to two wheelbarrow loads of stone or scrap iron at a time', and that 'the stones fly through the air in a cloud and then flog the ground with a force that can only be compared with that of pikes landing point-downwards'. Usually it took no more than two days' bombardment from this third parallel to sufficiently silence the defenders' resolve. It was Vauban's doggedness and determination which won through, and if the defenders of a city under siege knew there was little, if any, chance of a relief force coming to their aid, then surrender was the only course open to them.

One special technique devised by Vauban was for the gunners to direct their guns at a shallow angle of elevation in order that the projectiles would 'ricochet', thereby keeping to a minimum the amount of damage done to the fabric of the city. The term comes from the French word *ricocher* meaning 'to bounce', and it is believed to have first been used in 1688 during the siege of Phillipsborough in Holland. In this form of firing the gunners had to fire each cannon ball at an angle low enough to just graze the parapet of the wall, and send it in a bouncing trajectory into the interior of the defences. It required great skill and a steady gun crew to achieve this, but the result against defenders had an immediate effect on their morale because cannon balls fired in such a manner could inflict terrible injuries and even decapitate several men at once. An observer at the siege of Ath in Belgium in 1697 wrote that on entering the site:

> We found after the place was taken that the greatest part of the wounded had their arms and legs carried away upon the rampart by the effect of [ricochet] batteries, the balls giving the enemy incessant disquiet on all sides, following them even into their safe retreats, and dismounting their guns by breaking the wheels and cheeks of the carriages.

With this strategy Vauban had developed a simple, yet deadly tactic that would be copied by gunners in other armies.

VAUBAN'S FORTRESSES

The polygon fortress designs drawn up by Vauban, often referred to as 'star shaped' because of their design in plan view, emphasized the role of artillery in defence. Over the years he produced three different systems; these included Bitche in the eastern French region of Lorrain and Briancon, and incorporated the bastioned trace and massive designs using covered redoubts in the ravelins and recessed curtain walls with casemates. The casemate was a vaulted chamber set into the rampart and designed for mounting artillery, which could fire through a port. In this inherently strong construction artillery was virtually immune from the effects of enemy fire; in fact, the layout of Vauban's designs was so well defined that there were no 'blind spots' where the defenders could not fire, or where they could be exploited by an attacking force. The fortress at Nuef-Brisach, south-east of Colmar in the Alsace region, had defences that were deeper and wider than other fortresses. The artillery at this site was emplaced so that it provided overlapping arcs of fire to cover all approaches, and the integration with other weaponry made the site a formidable target if attacked.

The designs of Vauban's fortresses were technically superior to anything built before and they would influence military architects across Europe. An area within these new fortification designs was known as the 'terre-plein', from the French word meaning 'platform'. It was essentially an enlarged banquette behind the rampart, and was designed specifically for the emplacement of artillery: from here the guns could fire over the parapet. By the time of his death in 1707 Vauban is known to have been present at 143 engagements, including more than fifty sieges which he personally oversaw. As an architect he had built thirty-three fortified cities, was credited with fortifying a further 300 older citadels, and drew up plans for 160 other fortifications.

MENNO VAN COEHOORN

Vauban was not the only military theorist working in the field of military architecture. In

Holland there was Bernard de Gomme and Baron Menno van Coehoorn (sometimes written as Cohorn), both of whom developed their own thoughts on military architecture. Bernard de Gomme, 1620–85, travelled to England where he built the fortifications of Portsmouth and Tilbury Fort for King Charles II. Menno van Coehoorn, born in 1641, is often regarded by some as being equal to Vauban – indeed, he is sometimes referred to as the 'Dutch Vauban' – but he had ideas of his own, not all of which were necessarily practical. The fact that he was a contemporary of Vauban is not disputed, but Coehoorn would be one of the first strategists of his age to realize that siege warfare in the seventeenth century was little more than a prolonged artillery duel. Later strategists, such as the Marquis de Montalambert, 1714–1800, came to support that idea.

The skills of the two men were put to the test when a French army led by King Louis XIV laid siege to the City of Namur in May 1692. Known as either the War of the Grand Alliance, or the War of the League of Augsburg, it was an attempt by France to secure hegemony over the European continent. The war lasted from 1688 until 1697, and was conducted mainly in the area around Holland. At its conclusion France was elevated to primacy as a land power in Europe, and England emerged as a maritime power with artillery at sea. The defences at Namur were laid out in accordance to Coehoorn's plan, and when it became known that Vauban was to conduct the siege, military commanders of the day eagerly awaited the outcome. The Frenchman was older and had better experience, with some forty years military service to his credit. The siege began on 25 May, with Vauban ordering his usual series of saps and parallels to be constructed, which immediately invested the city and brought it under threat from several points. The garrison was well equipped with artillery, but unfortunately for them it was not suited to the task of defending their position.

For twelve days the siege was conducted using the tactics as formulated by Vauban. On 5 June the city surrendered and the two great men came face to face. The royal chronicler Racine was present at the meeting to record the moment for King Louis XIV. Coehoorn was observed to be angry and annoyed at the way Vauban had conducted the operation. It is more likely that Coehoorn was annoyed at himself for not realizing that Vauban was the better tactician. The garrison of Namur had expected to be assaulted from only one direction, rather than several points at once, and they believed that had this been the case, then the city could have held out for at least two more weeks. Whatever the case, however, the end result would have been the same. To add insult to injury, Vauban improved on the defences of Namur.

In 1695 these improved Namur defences were again put to the test when the city, defended by a garrison of 14,000 men under the command of Duke Louis de Boufflers, was besieged by an army of King William III of England. England had become involved in the war through the king's decision to provide support to Holland. The city of Namur withstood the siege for over two months before finally abandoning the site. What makes this action all the more significant is the fact that the Bank of England, created in 1694, had financed the campaign. This highlighted the fact that any war had become such an expensive venture that no one single monarch could conduct a campaign without the financial support of powerful money-lenders – in this particular instance, a bank.

Artillery positions showing mortars of carriages that also served as firing platforms. The gun shown is mounted on a carriage fitted with a false axle to improve manoeuvrability.

MORTARS

Coehoorn possessed the tactical skills for siege warfare and the talent to construct defensive fortifications, but unfortunately for him, Vauban knew more. Where he had the advantage over the Frenchman was in his knowledge of artillery, which went beyond its role in siege warfare. In fact his name has become linked to a range of mortars he developed. A mortar was a flexible weapon made from cast bronze usually mounted on a wooden base and capable of being transported on a wagon to its point of deployment. It is believed that Coehoorn developed the weapon in 1672, and that it was in service at the siege of Graves in the same year. It fired a shell weighing 24lb (10.8kg), and proved so successful that it was immediately adopted for general service. At the siege of Bonn, for example, in 1703, only one year before the death of Coehoorn, the Duke of Marlborough is recorded as having 500 Coehoorn mortars in his artillery train. The style of weapon designed by this versatile Dutchman would remain in use with various armies until the late nineteenth century, when it was still referred to as a Coehoorn or Cohorn mortar.

Mortars had been in service for many years, and their usefulness during sieges had long been recognized; indeed, Vauban and others, such as Count Schulenburg who served with the Venetian army, realized the importance of the mortar's capability to deliver shells filled with explosive directly into the midst of the enemy's positions. Most mortars were single-barrelled designs with calibres of varying sizes, but the majority were compact enough to be loaded on to a transport wagon and conveyed to its point of deployment. Mortars had been used during the English Civil War, where some had appeared with extraordinary calibres, between 10 and 18in (25 and 45cm). Around 1690 a French artillery officer by the name of Comminge developed a mortar with a calibre of 18in (45cm), and in 1700 the French also developed a multi-barrelled mortar called the 'Partridge'. The central tube

A type of mortar known as a trabuccho. It is identified from the location of the trunnions positioned near to the breech end of the barrel, rather than towards the centre of the barrel, but it operated in the same manner as the traditional mortar.

forming the barrel had a calibre of 4.3in (11cm), with thirteen smaller tubes around the circumference, each of which was capable of discharging a shell of 1.2in (3cm) calibre: a complete discharge of this weapon in one firing would have saturated the target area with exploding shells and caused considerable damage and confusion.

There was a version of the mortar called a 'trebuccho', which was readily identifiable by the fact that the trunnions supporting the barrel were set well back along the length of the barrel by the breech end. The trunnions on a mortar were set about midway down the length of the barrel, but both weapons were capable of being elevated to high angles to permit projectiles to be fired over walls at close range during sieges. The author of *A Light to the Art of Gunnery*, Captain Thomas Binning, recorded how mortars of the period were to be loaded and fired:

> 'Now he that would Load a Mortar-Peece, may elevate her Muzzle to what degree he will for his own conveniency; the Peece made clean, you put the Powder in the chamber, and upon the Powder a Wad of Rope-yarn, Hay, Or what you can provide; then you put on a turf of Earth cut on that purpose, that is large, wider that the vacant cylinder upon

> the Wad, which fills the Chamber, and then you put the Granado or other Fire-Work above that turf, and putting Grass or Hay above your Granado, that it may lie as you would in the Mortar, and also to keep the Powder in the Mortar from the fire of the Feusee…When you would discharge a Mortar Peece, first you must set fire to the Feusee of the Granado or Fire-Work, and you must see it burn well before you give fire to the Touch-hole'.

From this description we discover that the fuse of the shell was ignited before the weapon was fired. This was but one method, the other being to allow the flash of the propellant to ignite the fuse. However, such a fusing technique was rather ambiguous and the all-critical timing process for fusing would only be resolved with the appearance of the first watches that could be carried on the person.

THE ARTILLERY REGIMENTS ARE FOUNDED

By the 1670s a number of countries had recognized the need to establish professional regiments of artillery and incorporate them into the national standing army. Gustavus Adolphus of Sweden had pointed the way when he established an artillery force answerable to military discipline, rather than by the traditional method of hiring civilian contractors. He had established his army by drawing in every man between the ages of fifteen and sixty with 'no fixed abode', and to this strength he added more manpower by recruiting by lots every tenth man between the ages of eighteen and thirty. Other nations, such as Russia, were to learn and follow by example; however, the process of change was inevitably slow.

One of the first European monarchs to establish a standing regiment of artillery was King Louis XIV of France, who ordered an artillery regiment to be raised in 1671. This was a well trained and disciplined force from which future recruits could learn the practices of gunnery. In 1679 the king ordered that a military school be established at Douai, where all artillerymen would attend a course in gunnery as prescribed by the Master Gunner. Even so, he realized this was not enough, and in 1685 Louis XIV ordered that a special school be founded, for the study of artillery in all its aspects. The curriculum of studies included the instruction of the science of gunnery to officers. It was difficult to change the thinking of senior commanders, and almost impossible to break the habits of a lifetime. Nevertheless, through perseverance the changes were implemented, which eventually led to the realization that it was the only way to remain a credible military force. By implementing correct training procedures, wastage in ammunition and gunpowder was reduced, and this meant the artillery force could remain in action for much longer, which in turn could mean the difference between success and failure on the battlefield.

In England, the military planners realized that change was required. In 1672 an artillery laboratory was founded at Woolwich, which aimed to improve artillery technique in all its forms; this included proofing the guns, casting, and actual use in battle. In 1682 the artillery was reorganized, though it would not be granted the title 'Royal Artillery' until the eighteenth century. Despite these changes and improvements, English gunners and artillery design invariably lagged slightly behind European developments. Even so, it proved more than capable for the emergency that would face the English monarch in 1685.

Similar changes were being experienced all across Europe, from the Holy Roman Empire through to Spain, where several schools of gunnery tactics were established, and into Eastern European countries such as Poland. Uniforms were being adopted, and armies equipped with standardized weaponry. A structured course in military training and battlefield tactics was introduced. Armies were now professional bodies, and in future would take to the battlefield as well disciplined units, the officers trained to control their troops and obey orders. In 1690, the Duke of Wurttemberg-Neustadt remarked on the 'extraordinarily good Dutch gunners'. This positive comment highlights how the results of disciplined training were becoming evident to military commanders, and proved the worth of having special schools to learn the necessary skills for good gunnery.

Crisis on the Continents

The great landmasses of the African, Indian, and North and South American continents brought several powerful European nations into conflict. In the seventeenth century these vast areas, with their promise of almost limitless natural resources, were still being explored. These regions were known to have precious metals such as gold and silver, besides producing other luxury goods such as furs and spices, which attracted traders and settlers from England, Spain, France, Holland and Portugal. The financial rewards to be gained by exploiting these resources proved too much, and it was inevitable that fighting erupted between these rival countries as they sought to establish trade routes in these areas. As these European countries established colonies in these territories, the settlers also came into conflict with the local populace.

The native populations of these countries were never in a position to directly threaten the better-equipped European settlers, and were certainly no match for gunpowder weapons. They fought in a manner that was unfamiliar to the Europeans, who were more disciplined, and who, with powerful weaponry at their disposal, could engage such tribesmen long before they came close. Attacks by native tribesmen, therefore, tended to be directed against individual settlers whilst avoiding the blockhouses that were constructed to protect trading centres. The colonists exacted reprisals against tribes believed to have committed such attacks, but there were never any open battles in the form with which the Europeans were familiar. For example, the North American land that became Canada brought France and England into conflict. The French-engendered allegiance between the Algonquin tribe of native North Americans and the military establishment is estimated to have made available between 2,000 and 5,000 troops, mostly of a militia force. In 1686 when a request for reinforcements was sent to Paris, the reply merely stated that 'peace was desirable'. In other words, they had to make do with the resources available. Between 1655 and 1664 the Dutch fought three separate actions centred on Manhattan, Esopus and Long Island. The result was a forgone conclusion, and the local native tribes were left with no option but to submit to the Dutch.

Other European countries also fostered friendship with various tribes, achieved by trading metal tools and providing muskets in return for their support. Thus the English became friendly towards the Iroquois tribe, and the Dutch sought the Mohawk tribe to provide local knowledge. These two countries contested tracts of land on at least three occasions. The first Anglo-Dutch war started in 1652 when England seized some Dutch frontier posts. War was never openly declared in the formal manner, and the whole episode ended in 1654, the Dutch accepting the fact that they had lost the area of Long Island to the English. The second Anglo-Dutch war, lasting from 1664 to 1667, led to the Dutch relinquishing more territory. Four English frigates sailed into New Amsterdam Harbour on 7 September 1664, capturing Fort George, and the area became renamed New York. The third Anglo-Dutch war started in 1672 and was concluded in 1674, when Dutch forces temporarily regained lost territories.

In South America, native tribes such as the otherwise peaceful Pueblo Indians were attacking Spanish interests, and the fighting continued for twelve years. In 1680 the Spanish were seriously attacked for the first time, and the Pueblo Indians killed at least 400 soldiers and settlers. The fighting, mainly along the lines of guerrilla warfare, continued until 1692. The main reason for the war lasting as long as it did was because the local tribes refused to stand

Crisis on the Continents *continued*

and fight in the conventional manner, and the Europeans were reluctant to pursue the natives into the hills where they feared they would be ambushed. As the historians, R. Ernest Dupuy and Trevor N. Dupuy state:

> Unlike the nomadic plains Indians to the east, the peaceful Pueblo Indians were no match for even the weak Spanish military forces. They lacked military organization, and had no command system; they owed their initial success to surprise. Lacking metals, firearms and horses, they were outclassed by the Spanish…

When native forces were fired on by troops using muskets and artillery weapons, discharging either grape shot or canister shot, the effect was devastating. Lacking the knowledge and weapons to fight back, it was a one-sided contest. When the early Spanish settlers arrived in South America they had with them some pieces of artillery, and when attacked by local tribes such as the Aztecs and Incas, they opened fire with the guns. The natives had never seen the like before and, being deeply superstitious, believed that by throwing dust into the air they could hide from the deadly power of these weapons. Such incidents happened not only in South America, but also in Africa, albeit on a much more limited scale.

In India, European traders had established trade routes, and in 1609 King James of England authorized the establishment of the East India Trading Company. This continent, like Africa and the Americas, would bring European maritime nations into conflict; for instance in the 1650s English vessels fought short but fierce engagements with other nations such as Portugal. France also had a vested interest in the continent of India. Various local rulers had established powerful armies and built up artillery forces. Unlike the continents of Africa and the Americas, where the tribes were still living a Stone Age and nomadic existence, India had developed a great culture and was an extremely advanced society, attributes that lent themselves to European traders who sought to capitalize on this fact. Warfare involving gunpowder weaponry was a localized affair, though gun foundries were soon established. (*See* Chapter 5, Japan and the Far East.) This brought with it further conflict, which in the eighteenth century led to war between European countries such as France, England and Portugal, as they sought dominance across the whole continent. Artillery proved very significant in deciding the fate of this great country.

The same happened in the Americas, but there it was the colonists who revolted against the 'mother country', the rebels using the power of gunpowder weaponry, especially artillery, to carve out an independent state.

From this time onwards it could be argued that gunpowder was used to forge empires and establish trading routes that could increase a country's standing on the world's political stage, and whether at sea or on land, artillery was proving itself as the force multiplier in making final decisions. Certainly as countries moved abroad, it was the state deploying the stronger force that had the better chance of success. And this was the case in all the great continents.

4 The Years 1676–1700

TOWARDS THE END OF THE CENTURY

From 1650, gunnery was mainly concerned with improving the range and accuracy of all types of artillery. Most artillery at this stage was referred to by the weight of the projectile fired by the particular weapon, and it was now universally accepted to refer to the weapons simply as 'guns'. Inventories were still to be found that categorized artillery into four specific types: these included the culverin, sometimes called a culvering; and the siege guns and field guns of the types most commonly in use and which formed the main part of any artillery train. Within these categories could be found weapons called 'extraordinary' and 'bastard', their names indicating that they were not standard-sized weapons. There was also some ambiguity between the term 'siege artillery' and field artillery. Some countries believed that if one of the larger guns could keep pace with the marching army and traverse rough ground, it could be used in the role of field artillery.

The last category comprised the stone throwers, known variously as 'petrieri', 'brass basis' or 'petrieroes a baga'. These were weapons that fired stone projectiles between 2lb (1kg) and 150lb (68kg), and as such were an anachronistic 'hangover' from an earlier period. In fact by this time such weapons were outclassed by superior guns that fired cast-iron projectiles. Count Schulenburg of the Venetian army developed a mortar known as the 'Schulenburg perrier', designed to fire stone projectiles – the very name of this weapon indicated that it was a stone-throwing piece of artillery.

This was not the only instance when an antiquated form of weaponry was in use in the late seventeenth century. Some countries still had in service weapons of the early pre-loaded breech design, which dated back to some of the earliest forms of artillery. The main reason why these weapons were still in use was the financial cost of replacing them. Also, they may have been old-fashioned, but if they were operational, such weaponry had its uses on the battlefield.

Lastly, in some cases the new technology required to produce new and improved artillery may not have reached those armies where such ageing weaponry was still in use. In Japan, for example, the country had imposed virtual isolation on itself and would have been either unaware or unconcerned with continuing developments. Furthermore, weapons firing stone projectiles may have been all that was needed against some potential enemies. Certainly in the more remote areas such power gave domination over those weaker forces that may not have possessed gunpowder artillery.

THE OBSERVATIONS OF SIR JONAS MOORE

In 1673 Sir Jonas Moore published his book *Modern Fortification; or Elements of Military Architecture*, in which he described how barrels were manufactured, and the various calibres of artillery and their usefulness. In this work he details many types of artillery barrels, one of which he calls a 'Brass Basis' or 'Petrieroes A Baga'; it is illustrated alongside a device that he refers to as a 'Mascolo'. The brass basis is very obviously a design of an early breech-loading gun, and the 'mascolo' is the 'pot' holding the gunpowder charge for loading into the chamber. This observation reinforces the claim that old-fashioned weapons and modern weapons were in service at the same time.

According to the observations of Sir Jonas Moore the barrel of a gun was measured in terms of its own calibre. If, for example, the gun was, say, 6in (15cm) calibre and the barrel was thirty calibres, that gave it a length of 160in (4m) from the muzzle to the closed end of the barrel. An 'ordinary' gun had a barrel length of thirty-two calibres; an 'extraordinary' gun had a barrel length between thirty-nine and forty-one calibres; and the guns of 'bastard' size had barrels with lengths between twenty-six and twenty-eight calibres. Sir Jonas also described barrels as being 'small' to indicate that the tube of the barrel was not very thick. His term for a barrel with a thick tube was either 'reinforced' or 'fortified', while a 'common' barrel fell somewhere between the two.

Sir Jonas divided each category into subcategories in an effort to try and make sense of the calibres and functions of the guns. The culverin category, for example, he believed was 'to offend from afar off'. He listed these weapons in a range of types, and capable of firing a range of projectile weights '...from 14 to 30lb, although some do make them to 120lb.' His categorization shows the culverin as firing projectiles between 20 and 35lb (9 and 16kg), while the 'whole' culverin fired projectiles of 40lb (18kg) and over. Within this list of culverin types he grades the weapons as 'small' and 'bastard', with all their concomitants. The siege guns or 'cannons of battery', as he calls this group of weapons, usually had shorter barrels but with larger calibre. The 'quarter-cannon' fired projectiles between 16 and 18lb (7 and 8kg), the 'demi-cannon' between 20 and 28lb (9 and 13kg), and the 'cannon' from 30 to 50lb (14 to 23kg), with incremental changes in weight of 5lb (2kg) between the lower and upper weight limits. The 'whole cannon' fired a projectile over 70lb (32kg) in weight, with some capable of firing 120lb (54kg) missiles.

The field pieces he divided into four categories: the 'smeriglio' or 'robinet', which fired projectiles from 8oz to 1lb (227 to 450g) in weight; the 'falconet', projectiles between 2 and 4lb (0.9 and 1.8kg); the 'falcon' or 'half-saker', between 5 and 7lb (2.3 and 3kg); and finally the 'saker' or 'quarter culverin', between 8 and 12lb (3.6 and 5.4kg).

FURTHER INNOVATIONS

Armies were beginning to benefit from many new innovations emerging in this period. Not all of these new inventions had a direct application to the military, but it was only a question of time before they were adopted or modified to a military role. One such item was the introduction of the first timepieces that could be carried on the person. The ability to record time accurately had long been available, but only by means of large, cumbersome clocks. In 1675 the first watches that could be carried in a small pouch attached to a belt or in a man's pocket were introduced from France and Germany. Commanders could now synchronize the time of attack with other field commanders within the army, and make it possible for the artillery to open fire at a specified time without having to issue direct orders to that effect. Judging the time of flight for a projectile was now possible with such timepieces, especially for those fitted with a fuse such as those fired by mortars. According to *The Text Book of Ammunition*:

> The lack of any accurate time-piece added greatly to the difficulties of producing a 'time-fuse' in the sense of which we know the term... In the 17th century the repetition of the 'Apostles Creed' was one of the Proofmaster's favourite measurements of time, and though such a method may have commended itself to the orthodox, it could scarcely be said to have constituted a standard of accuracy.

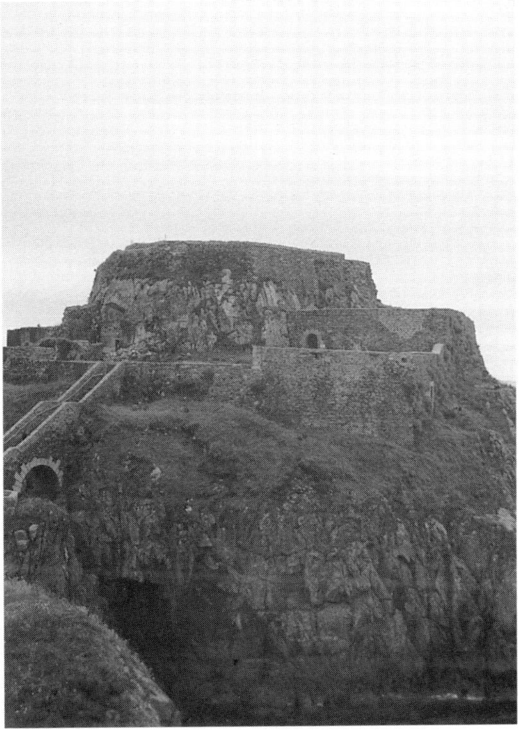

Specially designed platform where artillery could be deployed to defend the coast of Brittany in France against seaward attack. It remained in use until the twentieth century.

In other words, with the advent of watches, the ambiguity surrounding the calculation of a projectile's time of flight to the target was now ended. Fusing could now be gauged more accurately, and all the guns within a battery could commence firing at the same time. Time would become a contributing factor in winning a battle.

Gunners had long realized the importance of setting the barrel of a gun at the correct angle of elevation in order to engage the intended target. This setting was achieved through use of the 'gunner's quadrant', developed in the sixteenth century by Niccolo Tartaglia. Whilst it was extremely good for the role in which it was intended, gunners were continuously seeking improved range-finding techniques. With the appearance of the 'clinometer', gunners were provided with an alternative means of setting the elevation of the barrel. Exactly who developed this device and where it first appeared is not entirely clear, but it was certainly being used by some countries by the middle of the century. Basically, the clinometer was used to measure angles of elevation in much the same manner as the quadrant. However, rather than having to insert one of the angle arms into the barrel, the clinometer was simply placed on the top of the barrel. The required angle was set on the scale, and the barrel elevated to the required position. It was never intended to replace the quadrant, and the clinometer did not achieve universal acceptance. Instead, it really augmented the quadrant, and presented the gunner with a second opinion to satisfy any indecision he may have harboured on setting the barrel to the correct elevation.

Around 1687 the French army introduced the bayonet for use by musketeers. Bayonets had been in service prior to this, but were of a style termed 'plug' which referred to the fact that it was a wooden-handled dagger-type device. It was simply rammed into the muzzle of the musket, thereby effectively 'plugging' the barrel of the weapon and preventing it from being fired. The new style of bayonet was capable of being fitted to the muzzle of an infantryman's musket by means of a slip ring, which meant the musket could still be loaded and fired in the normal manner. The basic type of bayonet first appeared around 1647, and is thought to have been developed from a sword. Vauban, the French military architect and tactician, is believed to have ordered the introduction of this simple, yet effective weapon. With its introduction and further refinement, the role of the pikeman to protect the infantry and artillery from cavalry charges effectively came to an end. An infantryman with a bayonet fitted to his musket meant he could now serve in the role once designated to pikemen, and yet still retain the ability to fire. More men could now be armed with muskets, to increase the firepower on the battlefield and provide protection to the gunners against attack by cavalry.

Another design change came around 1680, when Antonio Gonzales discovered that by reshaping the powder chamber to a tapered form rather than the more usual cylindrical shape, the gun could take a much smaller charge without its apparently affecting range and penetration. This discovery opened the way for the development of dramatically lighter pieces; it also meant that gunpowder could be used more sparingly. This form had actually been developed around the area of Danzig during the fourteenth century, but was found to be unsuitable for firing large solid shot. Nothing more was done with this idea, but the design was later resurrected in Russia during the eighteenth century, when a whole range of artillery known as 'Unicorns' was developed for service unique to that country.

THE CHANNEL ISLANDS REVISITED

In military terms the Channel Islands have no real strategic value, but nevertheless as English possessions they had to be defended. Between 1678 and 1680 Colonel George Legge, Lieutenant General of the Ordnance from 1679 to 1682, and later 1st Lord Dartmouth, was ordered by King Charles II to undertake a commission and complete a military survey of the defences of the Channel Islands. Included in the report was the state of those defences on the island of Guernsey, formerly held by Parliamentary forces. Being an island of only some 25 square miles (65sq km) in size, most of the defences on the island had some bearing on coastal defence. At Fort Grey or Rocquaine Castle, Colonel Legge recorded that '…the battlements want some small repair to a new doore which will make it very strong'. The strategic position of Castle Cornet, overlooking the main harbour at St Peter Port, had had its defences improved, and there were now several sites where artillery could be directed to bring fire to bear on enemy shipping approaching the island from the east. Other

Castle Cornet on Guernsey, in the Channel Islands. The artillery sited here was used to defend the harbour of St Peter Port.

Castle Cornet protecting the harbour at St Peter Port on Guernsey in the Channel Islands. The Royalist garrison of the castle surrendered on 15 December 1651. It was the last Royalist stronghold to surrender, having been under siege for eight years and five months.

defences on the island are recorded in the Legge survey thus:

> Plaiderie (possibly Le Tour Grand) 2 × iron Sakers.
> West End of Town 1 × iron saker.
> Hougue a la Perre, Bulwark 1 × demy Culverin, 1 × Minion (in need of a carriage) iron.
> North of above: 1 × 6-pounder; 1 × iron Saker, Two extra demy Culverins were recommended: At the Key de la Viatte faceing to St, sans (St. Sampson), an iron demy Culverin.

At the bulwark Cotamanse, faceing Arme (Herm) and Jerau (Jethou): 1 × demy Culverin, 1 × Falcon, iron; 2 × 12-pounders were needed as well.
Belgrave Fort: 1 × demy Culverin; 1 × Falcon, iron. 2 × 12-pounders also needed.
Vale Castle: 1 × Minion; 1 × Falcon; 3 × demy Culverines needed as well.
Mont Crevet Mount: 2 × iron Sakers. 4 × 12-pounders needed as well.
Fort de l'Angle: East of Lancras: (On the site of Fort le Marchant): 3 × 12-pounder needed of ship carriages. It covered vessels approaching the harbour.
Nicq de herbe Lancras: 1 × iron 8-pounder. Another one was recommended.
Le Corbiere de Lancras: a musquett shot west of Nicq: 1 × iron saker. 2 additional 12-pounder were wanted.
Middle of Lancras: 1 × iron Saker. Instead there should be 2 × demy Culverins.
Near above: 1 × demy Culverins.
Near above: 1 × iron saker. Another 12-pounder was wanted.
Houmet nicol (on which stands Fort Houmet): 1 × Saker. 4 × 12-pounders needed as well.
Vazon: 3 × iron sakers. 2 × 12-pounders needed as well.
West of Vazon: An iron saker. To this should be added 2 × demy Culverin.
Rocquaine Castle: An iron Saker. This should be augmented by 3 × 12-pounders.

Colonel Legge concluded his survey with a number of recommendations for improving the state of the artillery on the island of Guernsey, and also for nearby Jersey. For example, in 1682 the destroyed powder magazine at Elizabeth Castle on Jersey had been rebuilt by Major General Lanier in the area of the lower ward. All in all, the islands were stoutly protected out of all proportion in relation to their actual importance. However, England could not be seen to be neglecting the defence of any of its territories, and therefore artillery had to be maintained regardless.

MOBILITY COMES TO THE GUNS

Heretofore the accepted method of hauling any artillery on its own carriage during a march was to pull it with the muzzle leading, but the developments initiated by Gustavus Adolphus with light regimental guns had shown that certainly light artillery could be harnessed to trails and pulled breech first by a team of two horses. In 1636 some Prussian states in the Holy Roman Empire had adopted what became known as the 'limber system'. This was a variation on the Swedish design, and involved hooking the trail on to another pair of wheels, thereby distributing the weight over four wheels instead of pressing down on just two. This feature did lead to a slight increase in weight, but this was to a great degree offset by the increased manoeuvrability imparted to the gun by the articulated joint. The device was being constantly developed and improved, and the design eventually evolved into the separate ammunition limber.

The heavier siege guns were still being pulled by the barrel, with men using ropes to guide and steady that part of the carriage being dragged on the ground. This part of the carriage was the 'trail', and rested on the ground when the gun was in its normal firing position. The role of these men following in the wake of the gun was to keep it on a true path and prevent it from overturning; to assist them in this task and make it easier to move the gun, a special fitting called a 'sled-foot'

Recreated seventeenth-century saker with crew. This was one of the basic field guns of the day, and served alongside other type of artillery on the battlefield. Note the tools, including swabs, stored on the gun carriage.

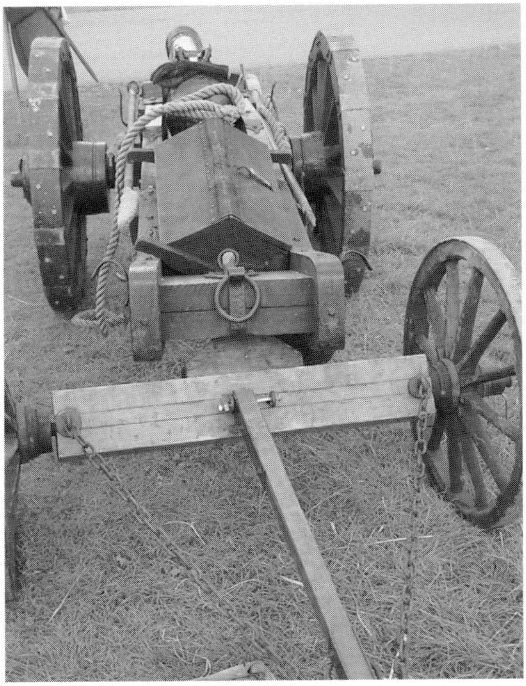

False axle as fitted under the carriage trail of seventeenth-century artillery pieces. This articulated feature gave more manoeuvrability to the carriage when it was being towed. The chest stored on the carriage is an ammunition locker.

was employed, which was shaped to allow it to slide freely over the rough ground. An account of its use in practice was written by Captain Thomas Binning, who records:

> This will be thought a new Invention, but I used the same in my Lord Middleton's Service from Aberdeen to Fyvie, where I caused them to make these Sled-feet, as you see fast to the carriage, in this manner; near to the Breech of the Peece there is a Bolt, whereon the end of the Sled-foot is; and under it, at the foot end of the Carriage, a Square-hack to lay over the Sled-foot; and a man or two thereby shall steer a Gun by a Height or Hole, in the way where she is drawn, so that many times it saves the Guns falling over. And when you are to meet your Enemy, or to make use of your Guns, you may lift up your Sled-feet, and lay them all along the side of the Carriage in manner as you see, on a Hack where they do not trouble, and unhacking the Ropes from the Hacks before, you may use your Gun at your pleasure.

Side detail of recreated false axle as fitted to artillery carriages in the seventeenth century. It aided manoeuvrability by making it easier to push the gun into position on the battlefield. Note the ammunition chest stored on the carriage.

It would appear from this description that steering a gun on the march was similar to a boat being steered by the helmsman at the tiller. It made sense to haul a gun muzzle first because it could be pulled into position and brought into action very quickly, as mentioned by Binning's account, and meant the gun did not have to be manoeuvred to face the enemy. The reference to 'hacks' appears to indicate fixing points to which the tow ropes were attached for hauling the gun.

Mobility of the artillery train was essential if it were to be deployed on the battlefield in time to open fire on the enemy's positions and cause confusion among their ranks. The speed with which it moved was still governed by the state of the roads and the fact that the gunners had to march alongside the guns and even push wheelbarrows containing powder and ammunition. By way of example, an artillery train containing 100 guns and 60 mortars would require 3,000 support wagons and 15,000 draught horses; the column could stretch back over 15 miles (24km) and take several hours to pass through one village on the route. By 1680 trail wheels were being universally fitted to carriages of guns to make their manhandling on the battlefield much easier. These were similar to the earlier 'limber system' inasmuch as the trail wheels were a special pair of wheels that permitted all types of artillery to be towed breech end first; this simple device was essentially a false axle that could be fitted to the trail quickly, and removed just as easily. It also meant that artillery carriages were now articulated, thus greatly increasing their manoeuvrability: the guns could now be moved with a greater degree of ease than ever before.

It took a large number of draught animals to haul artillery, whether horses or oxen, and it was hard work for them to move the guns; for example, it took eight horses to pull a two-wheeled wagon carrying a load of one ton. However, if four wheels were fitted to the wagon, then the load being carried could be doubled. It was this sort of observation on mobility that led to false axles being fitted, and harnessing the animals so they hauled guns breech end first. And having made this step, the way was now open to developing horse artillery, which would improve the speed with which guns could be deployed and moved about the battlefield. Furthermore in future the gunners would also ride into battle with their weapons, which meant that from this point on, the victorious army would invariably be the one that used its guns with the greatest ingenuity and audacity.

THE MONMOUTH REBELLION

When King Charles II of England died in 1685, his younger brother James Stuart ascended the throne in February that year to rule as James II. However, being a Catholic king in a predominantly Protestant country meant that he was never entirely popular, and his reign was far from quiet. He had been crowned king for only five months when he was confronted with his first real threat, and forced to defend his kingdom against an invasion. This was not from Holland or France, but was a rather abortive attack launched by James, Duke of Monmouth, the illegitimate son of the late Charles II, who believed he had a more rightful claim to the throne than did his uncle.

On 11 June 1685 James landed at Lyme Regis on the Dorsetshire coast in the West Country. He had with him a force of only eighty-two men, but he was full of confidence that he would secure the following of local Protestants. Alerted to the threat, King James despatched a force commanded by Louis Duras, Earl of Feversham, to intercept his nephew's army and destroy it. Monmouth was no stranger to war: he had seen service at the Battle of Bothwell Bridge on 22 June 1679, where he had defeated a Scottish rebel force during the Convenanter Rebellion. After consolidating his immediate forces, Monmouth moved inland, gathering a force that soon numbered 3,700. This level of manpower went some way to compensate for the fact that he had only four pieces of artillery in his army.

The king's army marched westwards in all haste to halt the usurper, but it is known that the full force of the artillery train was not deployed. Sensing that Monmouth would probably seek a campaign of manoeuvre and would prefer not to take up defensive positions, Feversham realized he would have no need of siege artillery or mortars. The artillery force that he had at his disposal included 'four iron 3-pounders and four brass falcons, together with their appropriate ammunition, carriages and equipment'. Without the encumbrance of heavy guns, the royal army could make quite fast marching time.

On 6 July the two armies finally met at the Battle of Sedgemore. Monmouth began the action by launching a night attack against Feversham's camp, but the approach of his cavalry force was detected and the royal army beat them back. Monmouth's infantry stood their ground, however, confident in the knowledge that the king's army numbered 2,500, therefore giving them the numerical superiority. But one of Feversham's commanders was John Churchill, a staunch Royalist and an experienced soldier who had learned part of his trade of soldiering in service abroad in Europe. His presence, and the fact that his troops were professional and well trained, meant that they were more than a match for Monmouth's well-meaning civilian volunteer force. It was a brief but bloody one-sided struggle – although the forces under Churchill did not have it entirely their own way, and at one point experienced difficulties in moving their artillery. The historian Macaulay recorded the fact that:

> …so defective were the appointments of the English army that there would have been much difficulty in dragging the great guns to the place where the battle was raging had not the Bishop of Winchester offered his coach horses and traces for the purpose.

Indeed, these animals were considered 'fitter for a bombardier [gunner] than a bishop'. Whilst the artillery train had been mobilized, these events indicate that, for some inexplicable reason, the organization surrounding its transportation had broken down. And this was not the only problem to beset the artillery before battle was joined.

Again, for some reason that has never been fully explained, the gunners to serve the artillery in the king's army were either absent, or not present in sufficient numbers to serve the guns. Unperturbed by this, Sergeant Weems of Dumbarton's, or the Royal Scots Regiment, took control of the situation and volunteered to supervise the firing of the guns, about which he had some knowledge. Monmouth's artillery could not equal the firepower of the guns in the Royalist army, and after Churchill had charged their position with his cavalry, driving off the gunners, they took no further part in the battle. It is unlikely that the problems with the royal army's artillery would have been a major setback for Feversham. It might have taken longer to subdue the rebel force, but with guaranteed reinforcements in gunners and weapons, the king's artillery force was always the strongest of the opposing forces. The rebel force suffered 1,500 killed in the fighting, whilst the king's army lost 500 men. Monmouth was taken prisoner and later executed, as were many of his followers in the 'Bloody Assizes' that followed the battle.

For his part in the action Sergeant Weems was awarded a £40 gratuity: 'For good service in the action at Sedgemoore in firing the great guns against the rebels.' Thus the status quo had been restored to the country by the use of artillery – but it was only a temporary settlement.

THE GLORIOUS REVOLUTION

The popularity of King James II continued to decline in England, and his reign became even more troubled. He was keenly interested in military matters, and in 1687, when trouble threatened in Ireland, he ordered quantities of stores to be assembled at Chester in readiness to undertake a campaign. On 5 June that year records show that James ordered a train of artillery to Hounslow Camp, which already had in its environs twenty-six regimental guns, six mortars and twelve heavy guns. The artillery train included:

> …2 demi-culverins of 12-feet long; 4 minions of 10-feet long; six 3-pounders of 6-feet long; two 3-pounders for the Queen's Regiment; two 3-pounders for the Princess's Regiment; two 3-pounders for Colonel Cornwallis's Regiment; 2 falconets for Sir E. Bute's Regiment; 2 falconets for Colonel Fulton's Regiment; and two 3-pounders for Colonel Buchan's Battalion.

In addition there were six brass mortars each of 7.7in (19.5cm) calibre mounted on travelling carriages – making this without doubt a most impressive train of artillery. In the event the camp was dismantled in early 1688, and King James never undertook the campaign in Ireland.

Attitudes towards King James continued to deteriorate, and on 15 October 1688 he was informed that he was under attack: '…a great and sudden invasion, with an armed force of foreigners, was about to be made in a hostile manner upon his kingdom'. In response, on 8 November he ordered a train of artillery to be mobilized in readiness to face this new threat. The invasion was headed by James's daughter Mary and her husband William of Orange, the Stadholder of the Netherlands. King James had created a standing army of 20,000 men and had a strong artillery train at his disposal. He moved westwards with the intention of confronting his son-in-law, but he only marched as far as Salisbury in Hampshire before he called a halt due to ill health.

James was becoming erratic, and his decisions were so unsettling to his army commanders that many deserted him. The result was that when William and Mary landed at Torbay on 5 November there were no opposing forces to prevent their successful 'invasion'. Unlike the Duke of Monmouth only three years earlier, this invasion was well equipped. The historian Macaulay records how William brought artillery with him: '...the apparatus he brought with him, though such had been in constant use on the continent, excited in our ancestors an admiration resembling that which the Indians of America felt for the Castilian harquebuses'. The artillery train, or 'apparatus', comprised '21 huge brass cannon which were with difficulty tugged along by 16 carthorses each'. This description places the guns in the category of demi-cannon, which would have had a calibre of at least 6.5in (16.5cm), and fired projectiles weighing 30lb (13.6kg) out to ranges of 2,000yd (1,800m).

This peaceful invasion was concluded on 13 February 1689 when William and Mary were proclaimed joint sovereigns, replacing the unacceptable Catholic James II, who had fled into exile in France two months earlier in December 1688. This whole episode brought stability back to mainland England, and also brought to pre-eminence the figure of John Churchill who had defeated Monmouth in 1685. Churchill was later created the Duke of Marlborough, and became the favourite military commander of King William and Queen Mary. His reputation increased during England's involvement in the War of the Spanish Succession, and it was he who introduced significant changes in the conduct of land warfare

The Siege of Londonderry in Ireland in 1689. This was a fierce and very bloody campaign involving religious beliefs between Protestants and Catholics. The deposed King James II of England tried to regain his throne, but the forces of King William III prevented this, thereby forcing James into exile.

and the tactics of weaponry, in particular the establishment of the 'artillery park'.

THE WAR OF THE LEAGUE OF AUGSBURG

Although King James had gone into exile in France, he was far from being inactive, and still posed a threat to the future of England. With the active support of his fellow Catholic monarch King Louis XIV of France, James was able in March 1689 to land at Kinsale in Ireland with a small force of French mercenaries. This action, and his subsequent campaigns, can be seen as the indirect involvement of England in the series of invasions that would become known as either the War of the Grand Alliance or the War of the League of Augsburg. At the time of his landing there were only a few Protestant areas in Ireland, including Enniskillen and Londonderry. However, the greatest single force was represented by a Jacobite army of 40,000 men commanded by Earl Richard Talbot of Tyrconnel.

On the 19 April the Irish-French arrived at Londonderry, a city with a population of 30,000 Protestants. The city's defences were served by only 7,000 men, while the attackers began to invest the site using the standard siege tactics of the day and deploying their artillery. At the same time the city of Enniskillen was also attacked by the Jacobite forces, and both sieges lasted until August 1689. During the siege of Londonderry a captain in the defenders' garrison recalled:

> At this time they played an abundance of bombs (the weight of many of them were near three hundredweight [336 pounds]) which killed many people. One bomb slew seventeen persons. I was in the next room one night at my supper, and seven men were thrown out of the third room next to that we were in, all killed and some of them in pieces. Into this city they played 596 bombs, which destroyed many of our people, and demolished many of our houses. Cannon bullets flew as fast as you could count them, and as soon as we took up their bullets we sent them back again post paid. Thus men, horses, and all went to destruction.

The siege at Londonderry ended when Captain John Leake broke through the blockade with a naval force, forcing the attackers to withdraw. The action had cost the attackers 5,000 men and the defending garrison had been reduced to 4,000 troops. Within days the siege at Enniskillen also ended.

It was the intention of James to regain his throne, but Louis XIV was content to use the war in Ireland as a sideshow to divert English troops away from Flanders in order that he might invade Holland. The campaign in Ireland continued, and a Scottish rising by Jacobite forces threatened the north of England. This took some troops away from the army of King William III, but never so many as to denude him of troops for other campaigns. The Jacobite uprising was eventually suppressed in a vicious manner, culminating in the Glencoe Massacre on 13 February 1692.

In March 1690, William decided to take matters into his own hands and personally led an army of some 40,000 men to Ireland. These were mainly mercenaries from across Europe, and at the time of their arrival William's father-in-law, the recently deposed King James, was in the north of Ireland having raised an army of 21,000 men. The two sides met on 11 July at the Battle of the Boyne. The fighting was fierce and devolved mainly into a cavalry action. At the end of the fighting James withdrew in good order, but with a loss of at least 1,500 men. William had lost 500 men but was able to consolidate his gains, and even send troops from England to Flanders, thereby thwarting the objectives of both his opponents.

The fighting in Ireland began to come to a conclusion following the Battle of Aughrim on 12 July 1691, where King William's army defeated an Irish-French force of 25,000 men. William lost only 700 men, while James lost 7,000 and so also the chance of any further campaigning, and finally withdrew back to France. It was now only the siege of Limerick that kept the campaign going. The city was held by Catholics, and was besieged by William's army and strong artillery force – but the besiegers had not had things all their own way during the operation. As the king's artillery train was making its way from Dublin towards Limerick on 11 August 1691 it was attacked by a Jacobite force of 500 horse and sixty dragoons. The artillery train consisted of sixty wagons with ammunition and 12,000lb (5,440kg) of gunpowder, 3,000 cannon balls, eight eighteen-pounder guns, and all the other necessary equipment for it to march and fight for three days. The Jacobite attack captured 500 horses and destroyed two guns and quantities of other supplies.

This was a blow to William's army, although it was by no means devastating. At Carrick his artillery train comprised fourteen 'battering pieces', 1,000 cannon balls for each gun, and 60,000lb (27,200kg) of gunpowder, along with great stocks of other stores. The city of Limerick was pounded by mortars and by William's great siege guns, though the defenders were well equipped with artillery. They finally surrendered their position on 13 October, and the king's army then captured more than forty-six guns of assorted calibres and sizes, including one bronze 48-pounder. The defenders negotiated terms of surrender that

The defences built to protect the harbour installations of Valletta on the island of Malta. These have been continuously improved and strengthened since the island was attacked by Turkish forces in 1565. Artillery was mounted at various locations to engage any attacking force.

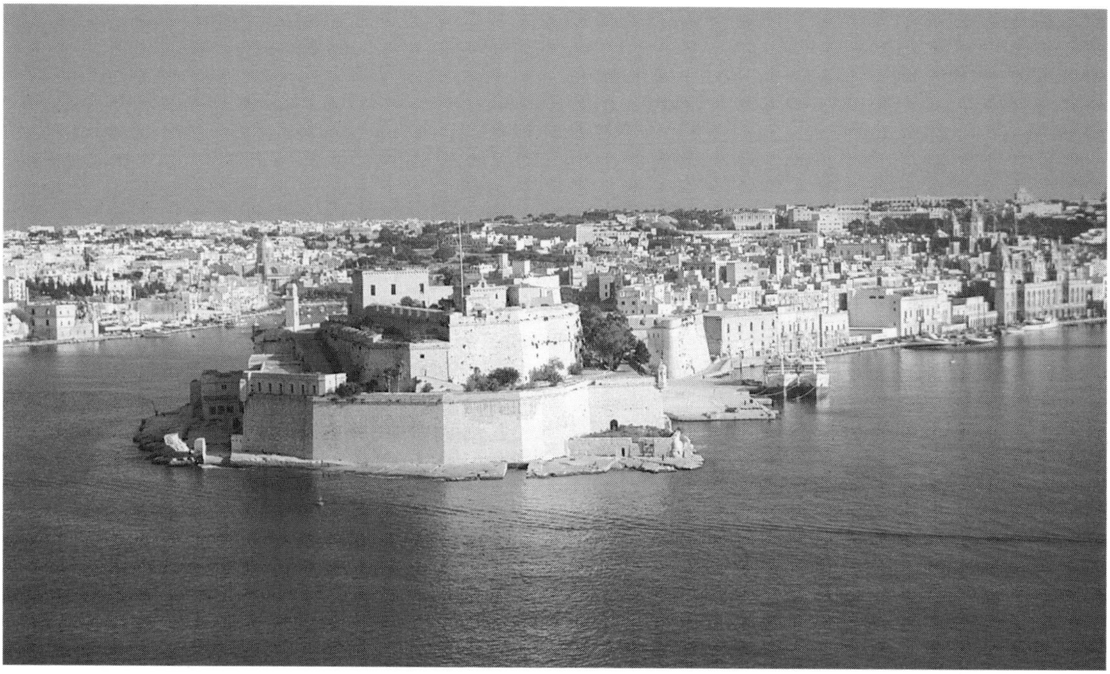

The harbour defences at Valletta on the island of Malta. They are extremely strong and remained in use until the twentieth century, having been the subject of a continuous improvement programme to permit artillery to be sited for coastal defence.

allowed them free and safe passage to France for those who wished to leave Ireland. Thus King William had kept his kingdom through the use of artillery, and forced his father-in-law James to withdraw once more to France.

Meanwhile the War of the League of Augsburg continued to be fought on mainland Europe, and at sea with naval battles such as the Battle of La Hogue, sometimes also referred to as the Battle of Barfleur. The French force was commanded by Admiral de Tourville, and had a total complement of artillery amounting to 3,240 guns spread across his fleet of forty-four men-of-war and thirty-eight 'fireboats'. Facing him was a joint Dutch and English fleet commanded by the admirals Edward Russell and George Rooke. There were sixty-three English warships and thirty-six Dutch vessels and a further thirty-eight 'fireboats', with a combined artillery force of 6,736 guns. The battle raged for five days between 29 May and 3 June 1692, and resulted in a resounding victory for the Dutch and English. Faced with such a defeat Louis XIV had to abandon any hope of invading England, and the engagement left the English in control of the waterways between the two countries.

King William was very much a leading military commander in the field, and as the fighting centred on Holland, he would remain a prominent figure; furthermore the actions of Louis XIV in revoking the Edict of Nantes made it all the easier for William to raise anti-French forces from Prussia and Holland. From its outbreak in 1688, the war had favoured first

Defences built for the protection of Plymouth harbour. These incorporate artillery positions and have been improved, strengthened and developed over the years from the seventeenth century.

one side and then the other. Naval engagements such as the Battle of Beachy Head fought on 10 July 1690 gave France temporary mastery at sea, and in the same year they made advances in land campaigns, such as at the Battle of Staffarda on 18 August. Luxembourg was allied with France, and on 1 July 1690 the army won an excellent victory at the Battle of Fleurus; but they were prevented from exploiting the fact when Louis ordered them not to invade Holland. With the threat to England removed, the war developed into a pan-European conflict, reaching down to Italy, Spain, Portugal and naval actions in the Mediterranean Sea.

On 29 July 1693 a force of 70,000 men led by William was defeated at the Battle of Neerwinden, sometimes referred to as Landwin. An army of troops from Luxembourg supported by their French allies inflicted losses amounting to 19,000 casualties on William's army, for the cost of only 9,000 dead and wounded. Again the Luxembourg forces were denied permission to pursue the retreating army, which, had they done so, might have led to England being pushed out of the war. Only at sea did the English gunnery produce any victories, and in July 1694 the fleet bombarded the towns of Dieppe and Le Havre on the north French coast.

In early 1696 England was once more threatened by French invasion, and the English fleet in the Mediterranean was withdrawn to prepare to meet this threat. In June the same year the Italian Duke of Savoy concluded a peace treaty with Louis XIV, who was then able to release an army of 30,000 troops to move northwards to face William's army, which was immobile in Flanders. Secret peace

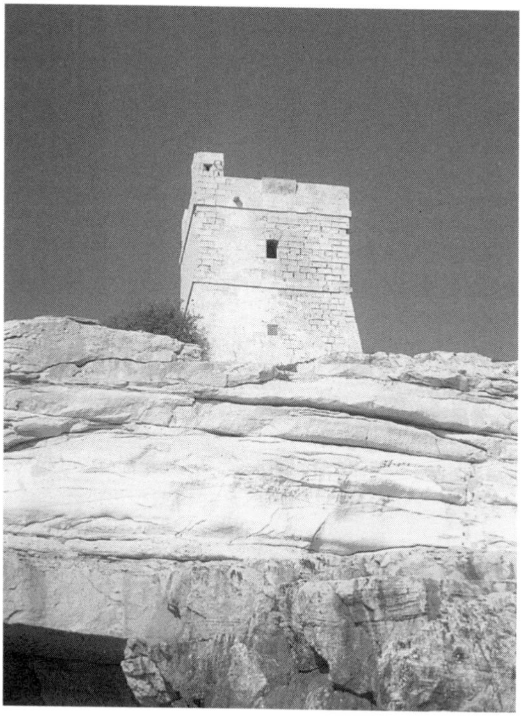

Seventeenth-century coastal defence tower on the island of Malta. Towers such as these were built to protect the island against attack and were armed with artillery mounted on the roof with gunpowder and ammunition stored inside.

negotiations were then entered into by various countries, which were, by now, facing the impossible task of providing more troops and money in order to keep fighting. Finally, and one by one, these countries accepted the terms laid out in the Treaty of Ryswick between 20 September and 30 October 1697: England, France, Spain, Holland and the Prussian States finally ended their nine-year-long war, bringing to a close one of the costliest wars of the age.

As the seventeenth century drew to a close, a new weapon design emerged, for use alongside existing artillery. It made its appearance in the middle of the War of the League of Augsburg, as did so many innovative weapon

An example of a late seventeenth-century howitzer. This weapon was being introduced just at the turn of the century, and may have originated in Holland.

designs, and over the next few centuries this new weapon added a new dimension to the use of artillery on the battlefield. Called the 'howitzer', it was known to have been in use in Holland around 1693, but the origin may be much older. The term 'howitzer', sometimes spelt as 'haubitzer', is generally believed to have originated from the Czech word 'houfnice', meaning catapult. However, most probable is that it was taken from the German Haupt Busch, meaning 'chief' or 'big' gun.

Howitzers were distinguished from standard guns and mortars by the size of the barrel, and the angle to which it could be elevated. Howitzer barrels could vary between twelve and thirty calibres in length – which is to say that if a howitzer was of 3in (7.5cm) calibre, the barrel would be between 36in (90cm) and 90in (2.2m) in length. The barrel of the howitzer could be elevated to angles between 45 and 80 degrees, which was steeper than the barrel of a gun, but less than that of a mortar. It would prove its worth in the battles of the eighteenth century, and become a versatile weapon in its own right by providing angles of fire between mortar and field guns. The howitzer was very definitely European in origin, and it entered service across the continent in many armies. However, it was not recorded in use with the English army until 1720, which only goes to illustrate that there was still disparity in artillery advances between England and the continent at the close of the seventeenth century.

By the latter part of this period it was obvious to all concerned that artillery had made amazing contributions to warfare, and transformed for ever the way in which wars would be fought. Artillery firepower had rendered the archer obsolete, and had also heralded the demise of the halberdier from the battlefield. Artillery in all its forms was now the absolute power on the battlefield, and its guns could halt cavalry charges, break up attacks by infantry, and inflict severe casualties at greater ranges across the battlefield. Earlier guns had increased the depth of the battlefield by the range of their projectiles, but the newer, more powerful guns improved on this. Artillery also added breadth to the battlefield, for armies were now deploying their guns across a broad frontage to cover enemy positions, and displayed them in battery formations to intimidate the opposing artillery forces.

Over the course of one hundred years artillery had been made mobile and more powerful, and it had become standardized. It had been used to establish national identities, maintain independence, create empires and trade routes, and even bring about the rise or fall of monarchs. Artillery had indeed become 'the last argument of kings', and during the eighteenth century, under the direction of forward-thinking military commanders, it would reach even greater heights of power on the battlefield and at sea.

Fusiliers: Bodyguards to the Artillery

It had been quickly realized that because of its very bulk, the progress made by the artillery train when deployed on campaign was hopelessly slow, and this made it highly vulnerable to attack whilst on the march. This weakness in mobility did not diminish when the artillery was deployed on the battlefield; in fact if anything, once the opening salvoes had been fired by the batteries and battle had commenced proper, the positions of the guns were more exposed to enemy attack. The reason for this was simple: as the opposing forces moved forwards away from their respective artillery positions, the guns were left exposed to possible attack and only protected by the gun crews themselves, who frequently lacked adequate weapons with which to defend their positions.

Some countries did make attempts to provide their artillery trains with a bodyguard to protect it against attack, but this move was seen as taking men away from their primary role on the battlefield. On the battlefield, artillery would usually remain where it had been deployed prior to the outbreak of fighting, and almost always remained in these positions for the duration of the engagement. At this period a battle invariably began with artillery firing against the opposing army; but as infantry units moved forwards, they became exposed to cavalry charges. Artillery positions made attractive targets, and were often subjected to attacks by cavalry. For this reason, military planners soon realized that in order to protect the guns, they had to have units specifically designated to defend them against direct attack.

Various measures were taken to provide the artillery with its own bodyguard, and one of the first moves was to raise special units known as Dragoons. In effect these troops were mounted infantry, and as such were armed with musket and sword, as infantrymen. Dragoons were not really detailed as the artillery bodyguard,

Fusiliers: Bodyguards to the Artillery *continued*

but being mounted it meant they could ride with the artillery train, but dismount and fight as infantry on the battlefield to protect the battery positions. During the English Civil War from 1642 onwards, both Parliamentarian and Royalist forces used regiments of Dragoons. Dragoons were used across Europe, and in England had been part of the militia force before 1628 in areas such as Cambridge and Ely. The muskets carried by Dragoon troops were of the 'flintlock' type, as opposed to the standard matchlock weapons that were discharged by means of applying a burning taper or 'match' to the priming pan. The matchlock musket was like a small piece of artillery, being loaded in the same manner and fired by a match. The flintlock weapon, however, was fired by means of a flint striking a steel cover to produce a spark to ignite the charge of powder. This dispensed with the need to have a continuously burning match. Flintlock weapons were

Recreated soldier of the seventeenth century armed with a dragoon flintlock-type musket. This was safer for troops posted to serve as guards with artillery trains.

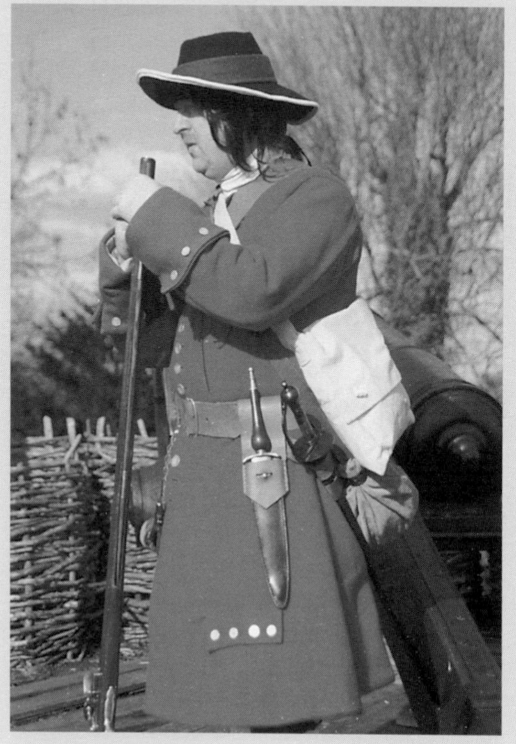

Recreated fusilier armed circa 1688 with a flintlock musket specially issued to such troops when guarding artillery. Note the 'plug' bayonet that could be fitted to the musket after it had been fired.

not only considered to be safer when guarding large stores of gunpowder, but were also more reliable in damp conditions. Flintlock weapons used by Dragoons were generally much shorter than matchlock weapons, having a barrel of only 16in (40cm) in length, which made loading more expedient whilst remaining mounted. These shortened weapons had the same calibre as a full musket bore, and became known as 'Dragons', a corruption after the troops who used them.

In 1671 King Louis XIV of France raised a new formation known as 'Regiment des Fusiliers', which was tasked with the role of protecting the artillery train and all its impedimenta, including the stocks of gunpowder. The troops of this new regiment were armed with short flintlock muskets known as fusils, which were much more expensive than the matchlocks but more reliable to use. The Fusiliers, sometimes written as Fuzileers, were well trained, and, being drilled as infantry, they were reliable troops. At around this time the Dragoon regiments across Europe were being absorbed into cavalry units, a trend that also spread to England. In 1673 the first such English unit to be styled as Fusiliers was raised at Bois-le-Duc for service in Holland as Sir Walter Vane's Regiment. The following year another regiment was raised at Bois-le-Duc, to be known as either The Irish Regiment or Viscount Clare's Regiment. Both of these regiments would eventually be transferred to service in England in 1688, during what was termed the 'Glorious Revolution'; later they evolved to become The Royal Warwick Fusiliers and The Royal Northumberland Fusiliers respectively.

The first Fusilier regiment to be raised directly in England was the City of London Regiment, King James II referring to the new formation as 'my Royal Regiment of Fusiliers'. Formed in June 1685, it was created by Lord Dartmouth from two companies of Tower Guards in London as the Ordnance Regiment or Royal Regiment of Fusiliers. It was the task of this regiment to march alongside and guard the artillery train, in the same manner as its French counterpart. However, James II was a Catholic monarch ruling a predominantly Protestant country, and as such was never wholly popular; by 1688 the country was disillusioned by his method of rule, and he went into exile in France. In the same year that he abdicated, another new Fusilier bodyguard regiment for the artillery was raised. This was Sir Richard Peyton's Regiment of Foot, which, after a series of changes in its title, finally became The Lancashire Fusiliers.

Over the next few years several more Fusilier regiments were raised in England, thus continuing the trend that had been set in Europe. The title 'Fusiliers' is understood to be derived from the type of weapon they carried, the fusil which had a flintlock action. The Fusilier regiments developed a distinct uniform that would distinguish them as serving in a specialized role. Later, however, military trends eventually saw a decline in the role of such specialized troops on the battlefield, as artillery became more autonomous.

Recreated fusilier of circa 1688 armed with a flintlock musket standing guard over his gun position. Note the gabions wicker baskets used to protect the gunners.

5 Japan and the Far East

Developments in artillery production in China around this period were also on the increase. This country was able to exploit its vast wealth of mineral deposits and manpower to produce some of the most advanced weaponry of the period. However, the country was not unified, and many regions, known as provinces, were at war with one another – in fact, some of these provinces were so vast that they could raise armies of exceptional size and engage in siege warfare against cities. The Dutch were among the foremost European trading nations in that part of the world, and by 1625 had established several enclaves on the island of Taiwan. It is probable that they also brought with them the techniques for improved casting and designs for modern cannon. Jesuit priests, a religious order of highly educated men founded in 1534, brought with them an advanced knowledge of casting barrels for artillery, based on European designs, which they were able to pass on as they journeyed into the expanses of China. Obviously it came at a price, either in gold or trade routes – but the fact remains that the knowledge of artillery was spreading.

With such guidance, gun founders in China were soon producing pieces of artillery with calibres varying from 5.5in to 6.3in (14 to 16cm); as such, these were classed as field artillery pieces. Even so, they still proved useful in sieges of cities, such as Mukden in 1621 when the Manchus forced the Ming from the Liao Basin, thereby leaving the city open to attack. Two years later a Ming army commanded by Yuang Ch'unghuan led his forces against the Manchu and defeated them using artillery either supplied directly by Jesuit priests or produced in foundries under their direction. In 1628, the Ming artillery was again instrumental in achieving another victory over the Manchu. But from 1629 the Manchu, led by Abahai, are known to have built up their force of artillery so that by 1634 they could face the Ming in open battle and on equal terms; and from that time the Ming began to decline in power, leaving the Manchu in the ascendancy. In fact the Manchu became so powerful that by 1660 they were fighting border clashes with the Russians in the north of the country. By 1685, the Manchu had forced the Russians out of their base at Albasin. Finally the two countries signed the Treaty of Nerchinsk, which brought about an end to the conflict.

OUTSIDE INFLUENCES

In seventeenth-century India European influences, mainly from Portugal, were very much in evidence. There was also some indication to suggest that Jesuit priests were also providing instruction on artillery developments. Some cannon were of extraordinary size, such as the huge 40-ton weapon known as the 'Moolk-I-Meidan', (sometimes written as 'Mukh-el-Maidan'),

Gunpowder weapons were used in Japan, but they were old-fashioned, such as this recreated early form of handgun called a 'hackbut'.

meaning either Master of the Field or Master of the Plain. It was probably cast at a site in Ahmednuggar around 1685 under the supervision of a gun founder from Turkey. Sometimes referred to as the 'Great Gun of Beejapore', it had a calibre of 28.5in (72cm) and was capable of firing a projectile weighing 1,000lb (450kg) using a charge of 80lb (36kg) of gunpowder. Unfortunately the range of this massive weapon is not recorded with any great authenticity, and it is quite probable that it was made as a symbol to show great power and wealth, and may never have been fired in battle.

Turkish influence was widely spread throughout India, and there are records indicating that Turkish gun founders were working in the country as early as 1548; they were known to be responsible for the casting of many great artillery pieces. It appears that the Indian princes had a penchant for large calibre cannons, such as the 'Great Brass Gun of Agra', known as 'Dhool Dhanee' ('The Scatterer'). This had a calibre of 23.5in (60cm) and, like the Moolk-I-Meidan, may never have been fired in battle. But these were the exception rather than the rule in artillery development in India at the time, and not all princes shared the same fondness for outsized calibres of cannon. In 1660 Moguls are known to have deployed artillery of more practical calibre mounted on wooden carriages that were capable of being hauled by bullocks, and used in campaigns against defences across Rajasthan.

In the seventeenth century, in the area we today know as Vietnam, there was an ongoing series of wars and minor skirmishes between the Trinh family in the north and the Nguyen family in the south. The Trinh family was far superior in weaponry and manpower. For example, they had an army of 100,000 men, a fleet of 500 vessels, 500 war elephants and an artillery force. Again, it was the Portuguese who came to offer advice and support; indeed, Portugal had been sending weapons to the Nguyen family for a long time, and since 1615 had even been supervising the gun foundry in the country. By 1631 the Nguyen had built up sufficient resources to go on the offensive and force the Trinh back: for instance at the naval battle of Bhat-Le in 1633 their artillery at sea forced the Trinh fleet to retreat; and at the Battle of Truong-duc, the Trinh lost many troops and gave ground. The war continued until 1673, with artillery all the while in much use. In that year the two warring families settled

Japanese armies used old-fashioned gunpowder weapons, such as this recreated early form of matchlock musket.

the border dispute and a demarcation line was agreed on, to give each side its own recognized territories.

Because the Far East is so rich in many mineral deposits, including copper and iron, the artillery pieces could be cast using a range of mediums, including the alloy bronze. With a plentiful supply of copper and tin, the constituent elements for bronze, it became the preferred metal for casting cannon barrels in the Far East, particularly for field guns. The use of artillery had successfully and quite naturally spread eastwards along the trade routes, and many oriental countries were soon producing guns of western design. In a turnabout, bronze guns would eventually be cast by Sinhalese gun founders at Jaffnapatam by local craftsmen for use by the Dutch East India Company in 1699.

JAPAN'S WAR AGAINST KOREA

Another country to discover the power of artillery was Japan, but, unlike its neighbours, the country followed a far different path. Despite its isolation, the various military factions in Japan at this time were familiar with gunpowder artillery and other forms of firearms. The country also had an aggressive overseas policy towards mainland Korea. In 1590, Toyomoti Hideyoshi, known as the 'great unifier', was the master of Japan, a position he had achieved through military victories on the battlefield and skilful alliances. By 1592, Hideyoshi dispatched an army of 200,000 troops to attack Korea. With their experience, strong will and better weaponry the Japanese inflicted one defeat after another on the Koreans, forcing them back to the Yalu

Because of Japan's isolation, her armies still used old-fashioned artillery, such as this recreated multi-barrelled ribauldequin.

Japanese culture and tradition valued the sword, and used basic forms of gunpowder weaponry such as this recreated matchlock.

river deep in the country. This overseas army had to be supported by a fleet of Japanese ships, bringing in supplies and fresh troops. In what amounts to an act of complacency, the Japanese fleet commander probably believed himself to be safe from attack. However, the commander of the Korean fleet, Yin Sunsin, took the initiative and attacked, using his armoured ships to inflict a heavy defeat on the Japanese fleet. This left the Japanese army cut off and subjected to guerrilla warfare by the Korean army, which by now was being supported by a Chinese army.

In 1598 Hideyoshi died and the following year his successor, Tokugawa Ieyasu, ordered the withdrawal of Japanese troops from Korea. Ieyasu was the 'last great unifier', and on the main island of Kyushu in Japan he faced a threat to his leadership by an alliance of the western daimyo commanded by Ishida Mitsunari. The two forces clashed at the Battle of Seki-ga-Hara on 21 October 1600, where the 74,000 strong army of Ieyasu faced a rebel force of 82,000 men. The Japanese warlord Minomoto Ieyasu had in an earlier period written: '...guns and gunpowder are what I desire more than gold brocade'. And so it was that the outcome of the battle was decided by a mixture of traditional warfare and exchanges of artillery fire. Through skilful use of his forces Tokugawa Ieyasu defeated Mitsunari, whose forces fled the battlefield leaving behind 40,000 dead. Fighting between rival factions and alliances of tribes continued for a further fifteen years until finally being concluded with the siege of Osaka castle between December 1614 and June 1615. During this six-month-long siege the castle was bombarded by artillery until, so badly battered, it finally fell on 1 June 1615.

Japanese troops used matchlock weapons such as this recreated 'pole-arm', more akin to hand-held artillery.

AN ISOLATIONIST POLICY

The fighting was at an end in Japan, but it was no time for great celebration, for on the same day Ieyasu died. He was succeeded by his son Hidetada, but the Tokugawa Shogunate had already been founded, and this dynasty would bring peace to Japan that would last for almost 250 years. In 1614, the Exclusion Policy had been passed to prevent interference and trade from outside nations. This was reaffirmed in 1637–38 with the Exclusion Act, which only permitted a small Dutch settlement at Hirado and a Chinese outpost at Nagasaki. To all intents and purposes Japan was cut off from the rest of the world.

It is understood that Portuguese explorers may have brought the first gunpowder and gunpowder weapons, including artillery, to Japan as early as 1542. This weaponry was demonstrated to the powerful warlords, such as Oda Nobunaga, who is known to have been greatly impressed. The introduction of such firearms into Japanese warfare, where combat was conducted on a ritualized scale more suited to the tactics of twelfth-century Crusaders, would have been a huge shock to their culture. The reaction of the first Japanese to be exposed to such weaponry must have been comparable to the Genoese troops two hundred years earlier at the Battle of Crecy in 1345, who, on being fired at by gunpowder artillery for the first time in military service, fled the battlefield. However, it was not long before Japanese warlords, including Oda Nabunaga, were having their troops trained in the use of firearms by Europeans.

At the Battle of Nagashino in 1575, for example, Nabunaga decisively defeated the forces of his enemy Takeda Katsuyori, who commanded an army of 15,000 men. He

Japanese troops used matchlock weapons such as this recreated 'pole-arm', more akin to hand-held artillery.

No new weapon technology was present in Japan in the seventeenth century, and the gunners used old weapons, such as this recreated short-barrelled veuglaire on a wooden mount.

joined forces with Tokugawa Ieyasu, and together they led a force of 38,000 men. Within this joint force Nabunaga had at least 3,000 arquebusiers (hand gunners), who were trained to fire their weapons in volleys. These troops and the more traditional warriors such as archers and those armed with swords killed 10,000 of Katsuyori's troops; or better than 67 per cent of the enemy force. It was through the judicial use of gunpowder weapons that Nabunaga and his successors eventually became the dominating force in Japan. The control of gunpowder weapons in Japan rested in the hands of the warlords, who implemented a strict control of such weaponry in an effort to promulgate the Samurai code throughout the country.

At the beginning of the seventeenth century the population of Japan is estimated to have been thirty million people. It was an extremely militaristic society, with some two million men forming the warrior class known as the Samurai, whose military code was based on use of the sword. But despite this militaristic attitude, the production of firearms and gunpowder was strictly controlled, so that even by the end of the

Japanese artillery was old-fashioned and very basic, such as this type of veuglaire recreated in the style of the period.

An early-style breech-loading weapon that equipped a number of armies in the Far East, where European technology in gunnery was often slow to reach. These weapons may have been old-fashioned, but they were still useful in battle against a less prepared enemy.

seventeenth century only a handful of armourers knew how to make and cast cannons. Even then, those cannon that did exist all dated from before 1620. As an island state Japan was more fortunate than European countries, and was able to centralize cannon founding. In 1607 all gun founders and gunsmiths were ordered to take their workshops to the city of Nagahama, where the four leading gunsmiths were elevated to Samurai status: this guaranteed their loyalty to the upper, sword-bearing classes. Orders for more gunpowder weapons could only be placed by the Commissioner of Guns, and only if commanded to do so by the state. Eventually the Japanese armouries became stock-piled with gunpowder weapons that were rarely, if ever, used and therefore did not become broken or worn out.

Japan had effectively introduced weapons control. The Shogun realized the power of gunpowder weapons, and sought to control it and instil a balance of arms. This status quo remained in place until 1854 when the American Commodore Perry with his 'black ships' appeared in Tokyo Bay and forced the country by threats of force to open its doors to the world. The country had seen the power of gunpowder weapons and turned its back on them, but with the arrival of the American fleet and at point of cannon, Western forces coerced the country to rejoin the rest of the world in trade. Because of its isolationist policy those gunpowder weapons in the arsenals of Japan were all antiquated and out of date, with little practical use on a nineteenth-century battlefield. Within fifty years of re-opening its doors, Japan startled the world with its ability to catch up with the leading military nations of the day. It then went on to show how rapidly a country could learn new tactics, and assemble modern weaponry on a scale that would allow it to forge out a powerful state.

6 Russia and Eastern Europe

Like the European monarchs, the heads of state in Russia were interested in the development of artillery early on in its history. Military commanders realized that only by developing an artillery force would the Russian army be able to protect the country against all invaders. As early as 1382, Moscow had been defended by Prince Dmitry of the Don, who used artillery to drive off the Mongol invaders. Military writers of the time recorded how Russian artillery was greatly feared by the Mongols.

More than 150 years later, between 1533 and 1547, during the reign of Ivan IV Vasilyvech (Ivan the Terrible), who ruled as the Grand Duke of Moscow, a professional group of artillerymen known as the 'pushkary' was established under his direction. This interest in artillery would be passed on and continued during the lifetime of Tsar Boris Godunov, 1552 to 1605, who established a cannon foundry about 120 miles (195km) south of Moscow. In fact, this armaments centre would continue to supply the Russian army and navy with pieces of artillery for the rest of the seventeenth century – indeed, it would continue to produce weapons until the Russian Revolution of 1917.

ARTILLERY TAKES A BACK SEAT

Unfortunately for Russia, at the start of the seventeenth century this pre-eminence in artillery was allowed to lapse, and this in turn affected the rest of the army and weakened the defence of the country. Russian forces at this time lacked proper leadership, which left them vulnerable to defeat in battle by smaller forces, such as those from Sweden and Poland. Russia could put thousands of troops into the field and replace all losses from a seemingly inexhaustible reserve of manpower. For example, in September 1610 at the Battle of Klushino, a Russian army of 30,000 men, including 8,000 Swedish mercenaries, commanded by Dmitri Shuisky, fought against a Polish army of only 4,000 men, commanded by Hetman Stanislas Zolkiewski and comprising 3,800 cavalry with only 200 infantry. The action was short but fiercely fought, and 15,000 men of the Russian forces were killed. The Poles then moved on to occupy the capital city of Moscow. From the results of this one action alone, it will be seen that it was not lack of manpower that beset Russia, but the absence of training, adequate weaponry and equipment.

Russia fought a number of wars with neighbouring countries, not all of which went in her favour. If anything, these early battles in the seventeenth century showed up the country's weaknesses, and the leaders set about trying to rectify these deficiencies. The bravery of the Russians was never in question, because in 1611 they rose up en masse and forced the Polish garrison to retreat from Moscow.

Russia at this time was also torn apart by internal fighting between factions laying

The Kremlin in Moscow, Russia. This formidable building served as an arsenal for the storage of artillery. The building has nineteen towers set within the surrounding walls, and each of these could allow at least two pieces of artillery to be sited for defence.

claim to the country's sovereignty. In 1605 one such brief claimant declared that he was Dmitri, the son of Ivan IV – though Dmitri was known to have been murdered years before. Whoever he was in reality, Dmitri was killed in a skirmish, but the episode serves to illustrate how such declarations only served to further unsettle the country.

Despite the distances separating Russia from the rest of Europe, news travelled fast, and men with military experience were attracted to the country, which they saw as a land of opportunity for soldiers of fortune such as themselves. One such soldier was General Patrick Gordon from Scotland, who joined the Russian army in 1661, during the reign of Tsar Aleksy Mijhailovich. At the time of his service Russia was battling Poland in a war that had already been three years in the fighting. This war continued until 1667, when it was concluded by the Treaty of Andrusovo.

The attraction of service in the Russian army drew many former soldiers, many of whom had experience with artillery, and who signed on as mercenaries. In the aftermath of the disastrous Russo-Swedish war of 1613–17, during which Poland also attacked Russia, the Russians actively sought to recruit foreign mercenaries for their military experience. This programme was instituted by Michael Hetman Chodkiewicz, and involved employing troops from Sweden, Holland, England and Denmark. He also purchased newer artillery weapons and stocks of gunpowder, and foreign troops set about training several Russian units in the conduct of modern warfare. But despite these moves the Russian army continued to display a predilection towards cavalry forces, even if it meant compromising the size of the modern artillery force.

In 1871, Lt Col W.L. Hime wrote in his work *The Mobility of Artillery*:

> The state of artillery was so bad during the latter half of the seventeenth century that it is strange that it did not entirely disappear from the battlefield. Field guns were almost useless from the difficulty of moving them… But while the artillery slumbered on in an undisturbed repose, isolated and unchanging, the efficiency of cavalry and infantry advanced.

He was obviously writing about artillery in general terms, but he may well have been referring directly to the Russian artillery in particular, such was its parlous state in the seventeenth century.

The fact that Russia had to purchase artillery from overseas illustrates how the gun foundries of the country had been allowed to deteriorate. Only the previous century Russian gun founders had produced the Tsar Pushka (Great Gun of Moscow) in 1586. This had a calibre of 36in (90cm) and the stone ball weighed 2,400lb (1,090kg). Although the cannon is believed never to have been fired in either anger or ceremony, it did nevertheless show what the country could produce. Now Russia could not produce enough artillery with which to equip its own forces, though fortunately for the country, future Tsars would remedy this failure.

Given its weakened state, it comes as a great surprise to learn that Russia ever went to war, and even went on the offensive. The army made positive moves in all directions as the country expanded, thereby bringing it into conflict with many neighbouring countries – and all the while Russia's fortunes see-sawed back and forward.

The Russo-Swedish War of 1656–58 can be seen as being part of the Great Northern war, which stemmed from religious intolerance between Roman Catholics and Protestants, and centred on the Baltic region. Much fighting occurred and led to great losses in the Russian army, such as the Battle of Riga in 1656, where they suffered 8,000 killed and 14,000 wounded and captured. The fact that the country continued to fight in the face of such adversity drew much admiration, and led to Daniel Defoe remarking on the military model to be found in the country. Even men without military experience, such as the English writer John Milton, were influenced enough to remark on Russia's stoicism: 'without order, nor willingly give battle but by stealth and ambush; of cold and hard Diet marvellously patient'. When one considers these words, they appear almost prophetic, and had future invaders been aware of such an assessment they may have rethought the consequences of their actions. It is interesting to wonder how different history might have been had Napoleon and Hitler known about these words and paid heed to them prior to their respective invasions of 1812 and 1941.

THE REIGN OF TSAR PETER THE GREAT

Perhaps the most radical changes to Russia's military forces were implemented during the reign of Tsar Peter the Great, who ruled from 1689 to 1725. He too followed the traditions established by his forebears, and continued to emulate Western European royal counterparts; like them he displayed a great and very real enthusiasm about his army at every level, especially the artillery arm. Early in his life Peter had enlisted in a regiment of artillery with the lowly rank of bombardier, and is known to have relished the hard work and duties that the rank held. He ate and slept by the guns with the crews, and took his turn in standing guard.

He reformed and modernized the Russian army, having learned many lessons the hard way during wars against Charles XII of Sweden, his sworn enemy. Throughout the entire period of his reign Peter maintained a keen interest in the artillery; during the Azov campaign of 1693 against Turkey, he personally inspected the artillery materials. Peter the Great also organized military exercises for training the army. One of the largest such field exercises to be held was conducted in 1694 and involved 30,000 troops, including cavalry, infantry and artillery. No live firing was conducted, which is to say no cannon balls or other projectiles were used, but nevertheless a high number of casualties was sustained with burns due to the blast of the guns. This army expanded Russia's empire, but at great cost, mainly at the hands of the Swedish army. When he died in 1725 Peter the Great left behind a country that was exhausted, but secure from attack. The army of 212,000 men consisted of experienced troops, who in turn were supported by a Cossack force of some 110,000 men.

OTHER EASTERN EUROPEAN STATES

Other eastern European states were also emerging militarily, and fighting to maintain their independence and fend off aggressive invaders. Unlike Russia, not all of them could absorb the severe punishments inflicted by defeat on the battlefield. One such country was Hungary, which made a heroic effort to defend itself against Turkey. However, the Turkish army of the Ottoman Empire, with its powerful artillery train and massive reserves of manpower, weaponry and equipment, was able to subdue north-east Hungary in 1682 and add the territory to their empire. The capital city of Belgrade fell to Austria in September 1688 following a siege of the city, which has been recorded in verse: 'An Austrian army awfully arrayed/Boldly by battery besieged Belgrade.'

This was a testimony to Austrian artillery, and the training of the gunners. Hungary would remain divided between Turkey and Austria as part of their empires until the twentieth century.

7 The English Civil War

During the sixteenth century artillery firepower had shown that walled towns were vulnerable, and that the vertical walls of medieval castles were unable to withstand bombardment, and this scenario was repeated many times from 1642 onwards during the English Civil War, when artillery was directed against many of the great castles across England and Wales, that had been garrisoned for either king or parliament. The situation between attacker and defender led to a number of siege operations in the old-fashioned manner. During this period England became virtually isolated from Europe, leading to a veritable stagnation of tactics at a time when European military theorists were advocating new designs in military fortifications and formulating new tactics for the use of artillery. The design of artillery itself was also being taken forwards to new directions.

The events leading to the outbreak of the English Civil War were deep-rooted in origin, and in essence came about as the result of constitutional differences between the king, Charles Stuart, and parliament, as to who exactly ruled the country. It was obviously only a question of time before such politics spilled over and set the whole kingdom aflame in open warfare. Some historians see the English Civil War as being three separate wars: the first was fought between 1642 and 1643, with a brief suspension before resuming again in 1644 and ending in 1646; the next, or second Civil War, was fought in 1648, and directed operations against Wales and the north-west of England; and the third or last Civil War was fought between 1650 and 1651, ending when Charles Stuart, the son of the executed King Charles II, left England for exile in Flanders.

THE FIRST CIVIL WAR

The Battle of Edgehill

By 1642 the political situation in England had deteriorated to such an irreversible degree that war became inevitable between King Charles I and parliament. The first battle of the Civil War was fought on 23 October 1642, when the two armies met at Edgehill, north of Oxford. The action commenced with the artillery from both sides opening fire in the usual manner. On this occasion the bombardment was inconclusive, and neither side inflicted serious casualties. An account written shortly after the battle tells: 'At Ege hill 16 peeces of Canon shot against 80 of E: [Earl] or Essex Liffegard & not one man hurte, & those 80 brake in upon 1000 of the Kings …' But that is not to say that either side could ignore the artillery of its opponents. At Edgehill the Parliamentary army sent a force of cavalry against the positions held by the Royalist artillery. The attack was successful, and the cavalry overran the battery, cutting down the gunners and thereby depriving the Royalists of experienced men

Robert Norton's list of artillery in service at the time of the Civil War

Name of piece	Calibre in in (cm)	Length in calibres	Weight in lb (kg)	Charge in lb (kg)
Cannon of 8	8 (20)	15	8,000 (3,630)	40 (18)
Cannon of 7	7 (18)	16	7,000 (3,175)	25 (11)
Demi-cannon	6.5 (16.5)	18	6,000 (2,720)	20 (9)
Culvering	5.5 (14)	28	4,500 (2,040)	15 (7)
Demi-culvering	4.5 (11)	32	2,500 (1,135)	9 (4)
Saker	3.5 (9)	36	1,500 (680)	5.25 (2.4)
Minion	3.25 (8)	30	1,200 (545)	3.25 (1.5)
Falcon	2.75 (7)	42	700 (320)	2.5 (1)
Falconet	2.25 (6)	48	500 (230)	1.25 (0.5)
Cannon-perrier	9/10/12 (23/25/28)	8	3,500 (1,590)	3/3.5/4 (1.3/1.6/1.8)
Demi-cannon-drake	6.5 (16.5)	16	3,000 (1,360)	9 (4)
Culvering-drake	5.5 (14)	16	2,000 (907)	5 (2.2)
Demi-culvering-drake	4.5 (11)	16	1,500 (680)	3.5 (1.6)
Saker-drake	3.5 (9)	18	1,200 (545)	2 (0.9)

and reducing the number of guns which could participate further in the battle.

At the end of the battle at about 6pm, both sides claimed victory. It had been a hard-fought action, with the armies beginning to run short of powder and ammunition. The Parliamentarian army had managed to bring up some reserves just before the fighting stopped, and the armies moved away from one another. Over the next few days each side made plans to march towards London. To lighten his load for the journey the king abandoned his artillery, which was seized by the Parliamentarian forces. It was an ill-advised decision.

The Parliamentarian army reached the city first, and when the king arrived at the outskirts on 12 November, the citizens there were hostile to his forces. On 13 November the 'trained bands', or 'militia', attacked the king's army, forcing it to withdraw. The city was not his, and the Royalist army had to fall back on Oxford, from where the king planned his next move. Any equipment lost was difficult enough to replace, but artillery was virtually impossible to replace because the Parliamentarians had seized all the gun foundry centres in England. The Parliamentarian commander, the Earl of Denbigh, was one of the few leaders who realized the true importance of artillery, and declared that he would 'rather lose ten lives than one piece of my artillery'.

In 1643, one of 'His Majesties Gunners', Robert Norton, who had written *The Gunner shewing the Whole Practice of Artillery* published in 1628, compiled a list of artillery in service at the time of the Civil War. These weapons would have been available to both sides, but in varying quantities. He dedicated his work to the Duke of Buckingham, an adviser to King Charles I. The list is reproduced in the table here above.

Artillery Proves its Worth

Royalist artillery did not always display the same poor standard as at Edgehill, and could,

An artist's impression of Oliver Cromwell on horseback at the Battle of Marston Moor, 2 July 1644. Note the large cannon to the left of the picture, which could be a representation of a saker, which was in use at the time.

when given the opportunity, prove its true worth. During the engagement at Bradock Down, on 19 January 1643, the guns provided fire support to the cavalry, which led to them inflicting heavy loss on the Parliamentarian forces and capturing five pieces of artillery. On 13 July 1643, during an engagement at Roundway Down, the Royalists' guns were so well handled that they were once more able to support the cavalry and enable the king's troops to seize a number of guns from the Parliamentarians' positions, and to open fire with them against their former owners.

Some actions saw only an exchange of desultory artillery fire, but other engagements during the Civil War opened with a heavy exchange of artillery. For example, on 2 July 1644, at the Battle of Marston Moor, where the Parliamentarians had twenty-five guns, the opening bombardment was relatively ineffectual. Nevertheless the potential firepower from twenty-eight guns fielded by the Royalist army still remained a major threat to the Parliamentarian army. The artillery positions were attacked

The moment of firing a recreated drake minion, a type of weapon used during the English Civil War. This was a field piece, but it could be used during siege operations against castles and walled cities.

by Cromwell's troops coming in from the flank, and they captured the guns. The battle cost the king's army 4,000 casualties, and was a defeat from which it never fully recovered.

Many observations would be made on the subject of artillery and its efficacy during the English Civil War. On its own artillery could not produce victories, but on the battlefield, especially at close quarters, it could inflict heavy casualties. Apart from the spherical solid iron shot or ball, artillery could fire case or canister shot. This load consisted of dozens of musket balls contained within a tin case or canister, hence its term; when fired they were discharged like a giant shotgun. At a range of 200yd (183m), the effect against cavalry was devastating and guaranteed to break up most charges. One particular record, written by Colonel Slingsby, almost certainly refers to the effect of canister shot when he observed 'legs and arms flying apace' when infantry was fired on by artillery at a range of 200yd (183m). Other accounts concerning artillery fire inflicting casualties include that written by Captain Gwynne, who saw: 'A whole file of men, six deep, with their heads struck off with one cannon shot of ours.' George Creighton, chaplain to Lord Ormonde's regiment, described the effect of artillery fire at the Battle of Ross, Wexford, in March 1647: 'I did see what terrible work the ordnance had made, what goodly men and horses lay there all torn, and their guts lying on the ground, arms cast away, and strewn all over the field.'

Naming Weapons

On a lighter note, but in keeping with the age-old military tradition of 'dark humour', the gunners on both sides bestowed names on their weapons. The gunners in the Parliamentary regiment of Sir John Meldum, despite their Puritan ideals, nicknamed their largest artillery piece, a thirty-two-pounder of 12ft (3.6m) in length, 'Sweet Lips' after a well-known woman of ill repute in Hull. Two demi-cannon in the artillery force of the Earl of Newcastle were known by the names of 'Gog' and 'Magog'; both were used at the Battle of Adwalton Moor on 30 June 1643. There was also the mortar 'Roaring Meg' used in the siege of Raglan Castle, and another by the same name used at Hopton Heath on 19 March 1643. Such titles were given to the weapons by the gunners, who viewed their weapons with the same level of familiarity as a cavalryman might favour his horse.

The Military Leaders

Both sides in the English Civil War had commanders who had seen extensive military action during various European wars. For example, Sergeant Major General Lord Astley was a professional soldier serving in the king's army, and had seen service in Denmark, Holland and Prussia. Sir William Waller, although not perhaps the most capable of commanders in the Parliamentarian army, had seen service in the Venetian army and fought during the Thirty Years War. The King's Master of Ordnance was Mountjoy Blount, Earl of Newport, a position he had held since 1634. However, daily operations of the Ordnance Office were the responsibility of a Lieutenant of the Ordnance, and this position was held by various persons. In the Parliamentarian army at the time of the Battle of Edgehill the office of General of Ordnance was held by Henry Mordaunt, Earl of Peterborough, with Philibert Du Bois serving as the effective commander of artillery, with the rank of Lieutenant General of Ordnance.

Common types of artillery in 1646							
Weapon	Weight of shot	Calibre	Weight of charge	Weight of piece	Number of men to to draw	Number of horses to draw	Maximum range
Cannon Royal	63lb (29kg)	8in (20cm)	40lb (18kg)	8,008lb (3,630lb)	90	16	1,500yd(1,370m)
Cannon	47lb (21kg)	7in (18cm)	34lb (15kg)	6,944lb (3,150kg)	70	12	1,740yd (1,591m)
Demi-cannon	27lb (12.2kg)	6in (15cm)	25lb (11.3kg)	5,992lb (2,719kg)	60	10	1,600yd (1,460m)
Culverin	15lb (6.8kg)	5in (13cm)	18lb (8kg)	4,592lb (2,080kg)	50	8	2,000yd (1,830m)
Demi-Culverin	9lb (4kg)	4.5in (11cm)	9lb (4kg)	2,498lb (1,133kg)	36	7	1,800yd (1,650m)
Saker and Drake	5lb (2kg)	3.5in (9cm)	5lb (2kg)	1,600lb (726kg)	24	5	1,500yd (1,370m)
Minion	3.7lb (1.7kg)	3in (8cm)	3.5lb (1.6kg)	1,176lb (533kg)	20	4	1,400yd (1,280m)
Falcon	2.5lb (1kg)	2.7in (6.8cm)	2.5lb (1kg)	695lb (315kg)	16	2	1,200yd (1,100m)

Artillery in the 1640s

In 1646, four years after the start of the English Civil War, one authority records that artillery of the period in England at that time ranged from cannon royal, through cannon, demi-cannon, fifteen-pounder culverin, demi-culverin, six-pounder saker, minion, falcon and falconet, down to the small robinet. The writer would no doubt have realized that such an inventory of different calibres of weapon would have caused problems regarding re-supply – though admittedly some of these pieces may have had very limited or localized usage. An examination of these lists reveals there were some nineteen different types of artillery being used in England at the time, ranging from the massive 'syren' weighing 8,100lb (3,675kg) down to the small 'base' of 450lb (204kg). The most commonly used types however, were the above:

The English Civil War is generally seen by many as a series of cavalry actions supported by infantry units armed with matchlock muskets or pikes of 16ft (5m) in length and formed into blocks. It could be argued that artillery had little decisive effect, except at a handful of engagements, and historians vary in their opinion as to its usefulness during the English Civil War. Richard Garret, for example, states: 'All one could say about the artillery was that they had guns. Since these weapons seldom managed to get the range right, and since they were badly built, they did small execution.' In his book *Artillery Through The Ages*, Colonel H.C.B. Rogers makes the opposite statement, claiming: 'Artillery played

The Battle of Preston fought on 17 August 1648. The fighting lasted four hours, and ended with the Parliamentarian army commanded by Oliver Cromwell defeating a Royalist army. Thus ended the Second Civil War.

a prominent part in the Civil War …, though in siege warfare rather than in field operations.' A third historian, Field Marshal Lord Carver, in his book *The Seven Ages of the British Army*, states that:

> In a typical battle, the first exchange of fire would be from the artillery, aimed at breaking up the enemy's battle line. However, it does not seem to have been very effective and in some cases, for instance the Battle of Preston [17–19 August 1648] neither side had any artillery as it had failed to keep up.

It will be noticed that these statements vary in opinion, as did the belief of the gunners at the time, who did not always place a great deal of trust in the reliability of their weapons. For example, Royalist artillerymen held the opinion that 'The first shot [was] for the devil, the second for God, and the third for the king.'

Certainly artillery was placed low in the order of priority by both sides in the early days of the war, but wherever it was present during open battle or at a siege, the artillery did take part in the action. Artillery, it must be said, was not always handled with great precision and dexterity, and its success or failure during actions fell to the relationship between the General of Artillery and the Commander-in-Chief of the army. For example, if the artillery commander knew that cavalry and infantry would support his forces, the guns could be deployed in a more open order across the battlefield to fire on a broad frontage. If, on the other hand, support was not forthcoming, the artillery would have to be placed more closely together, for mutual support. Light guns or field pieces were usually positioned in batteries forward of the main body of troops, and if time permitted, the gunners would construct earthen defences.

Royalist Forces are Routed

In late 1642 an action at Southam, Warwick, which had begun as a small-scale cavalry engagement, turned into a rout of the Royalist forces. It was described by Sergeant Nehemiah Wharton of the Parliamentarian forces, commanded by Robert Devereux, Earl of Essex:

> Monday morninge wee marched into Warwickshire… until wee came to Southam… in the morninge early our enemies consisting of about eight hundred horse and three hundred foote, with ordinance led by the Earl of Northampton, the Lord of Carnavon, and the Lord Compton… intended to set upon us before wee could gather our companies together, but beinge ready all night, early in the morninge wee went to meet them with a few troopes of horse and six field pieces, and being on fier to be at them wee marched thorou the coarn and got to the hill of them, but they came short. Our gunner tooke theire owne bullet, sent it to them againe and killed a man and a horse. After, wee gave them 8 shott more, whereupon all theire foote companies fled and offered theire armies in the townes adjacent for twelve pence apiece.

Oliver Cromwell, the Parliamentarian commander, quickly learned the art of warfare and, in particular, the use of artillery. He realized the usefulness of the artillery, especially in siege warfare against castles.

Some credit the above account to one of the Earl of Essex's subalterns, but the name of Sergeant Nehemiah Wharton is strongly attached to the writing. What the account does tell us is that when caught by spirited fighting forces supported by artillery, one side, in this case the Royalists, would often run away. On this particular occasion, so desperate were they to depart and lighten their load, that the troops even tried to sell their firearms for the modern equivalent of five pence. Four years later, at Rowton Heath on 24 September 1646, it was the turn of the Royalist artillery to unsettle the Parliamentarian forces, when a single gun fired a 29lb (13kg) ball against an infantry regiment and '…made such a line through them that they had little mind to close again'.

Oliver Cromwell, Parliamentarian Leader

One commander of the Parliamentarian army who would emerge as the natural leader was Oliver Cromwell. Despite his lack of formal military training he was astute enough to learn the rules of warfare 'in the saddle', as it were. Whilst the Parliamentarian army won victories, these were quite costly in terms of casualties, and the troops lacked adequate training. Cromwell realized this, and with the support of other commanders, such as Sir William Waller, a force known as the New Model Army was raised.

The New Model Army of the Parliamentary forces came into being on 15 February 1645, with Sir Thomas Fairfax in command and

The Battle of Naseby was fought on 14 June 1645. Cavalry forces commanded by Oliver Cromwell produced a victory for the Parliamentarian army and captured the artillery of the Royalist army.

Oliver Cromwell as the Lieutenant General of Horse. The original strength of the force was 22,000 men formed into various units and regiments. There were 14,400 infantry formed into twelve regiments each, with 1,200 men and 7,600 mounted formed into eleven regiments each of 600 men, and one regiment of Dragoons with 1,000 men.

This left the artillery ignored and without personnel who could be trained, and the situation was only resolved as the New Model Army gained strength. Indeed, it was some time before the artillery arm of the Parliamentary forces was given the recognition it deserved. The guns tended to be older, heavier weapons more suited to siege warfare against walled towns or where garrisons had taken over castles. There had never been a standing artillery force in England, and it had been left to the Ordnance Department to raise 'trains' of artillery with hired horses and civilian drivers along with other supporting services. Artillery trains, at the time of the English Civil War, were not of a consistent size, being assembled from whatever weaponry was available. A complete reorganization was obviously needed on both sides, but it was only the likes of Cromwell who realized the necessity of such a move.

At the beginning of the war the Royalist army was at a distinct disadvantage in the numbers of artillery pieces, and with every defeat the king's army lost more artillery. It was only by capturing the enemy's guns – such as the forty-nine taken at the Battle of Lostwithiel in September 1644 – along with one hundred barrels of powder and 5,000 muskets, that the Royalist army and artillery was able to remain a capable force in the field.

The New Model Army, 1645

When the New Model Army marched out on campaign in April 1645 it was more disciplined and better equipped than any other army that had ever before taken to the battlefield: it was a properly trained force that was

Old Wardour Castle in Wiltshire was besieged by a Parliamentarian force that deployed artillery against the garrison in 1643.

more than a match for anything the Royalist army could pit against it. Furthermore the artillery train was eventually reorganized to a scale that matched the rest of the New Model Army: by the end of the first Civil War in 1646 it numbered some fifty-six weapons, comprising sixteen demi-culverins, ten sakers, fifteen drakes and fifteen smaller field pieces, and required over 1,000 horses for transport. This figure did not include the large-calibre cannons and mortars that would be brought forward for siege operations. For protection whilst on the march the artillery train had assigned to it two companies of musketeers, armed with flintlock muskets and detailed to act as bodyguards.

Whilst field artillery had an important role in open warfare, the very large guns were indispensable during siege operations at the important sites of Bristol, Leicester, Leeds, Worcester and Lincoln. An average artillery piece could fire fifteen shots an hour, and whilst ranges of 2,000yd (1,830m) could be achieved, accuracy beyond 300yd (274m) was not precise. In view of this, it is no wonder that commanders were more inclined to save artillery for use during sieges where its firepower yielded better results; even at lesser siege operations artillery could be deployed.

The Siege of Old Wardour Castle

One such relatively small-scale siege that escalated out of all initial expectations was the operation directed against Old Wardour Castle in Wiltshire, held by Lady Blanche, the sixty-year old wife of Sir Thomas, second Lord Arundell, who was in Oxford campaigning with the king. In April 1643, the castle was defended by a garrison of twenty-five, including female servants, when a Parliamentarian force of some 700 horse, commanded by Sir Edward Hungerford, approached the site and took up positions. Sir Edward assessed the situation and decided it warranted reinforcements and artillery support. A force of 1,300 men arrived, supported by two cannons, and for several days the castle came under sporadic fire from the guns. The artillery fire was light and succeeded in causing little damage,

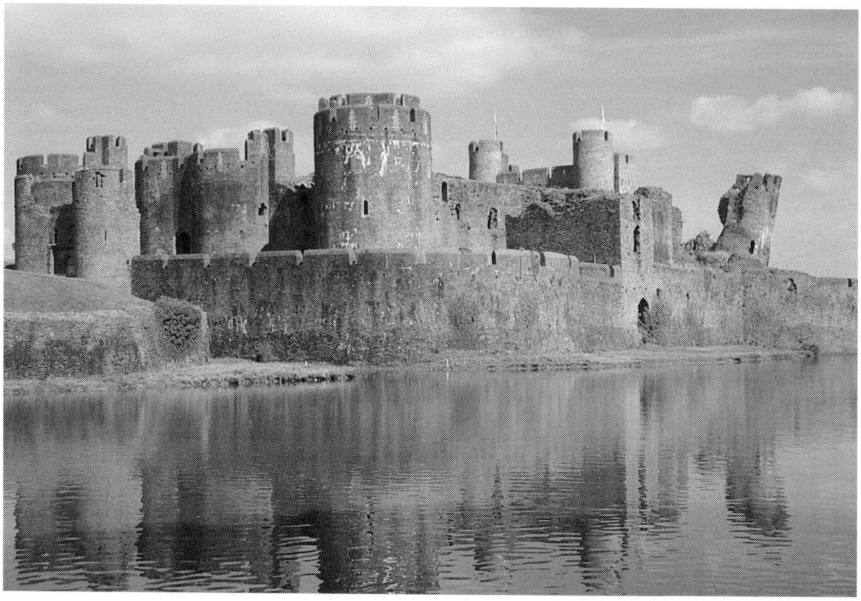

Caerphilly Castle in Wales at one time counted artillery in its defences, but during the English Civil War it was never besieged. When it was evacuated in 1646 a Royalist force destroyed parts of the defences using charges of gunpowder.

apart from bringing down one chimneypiece and breaking all the glass in the windows.

The castle was completely surrounded by superior forces, and there was no chance of a relief force coming to the aid of the defenders. Lady Blanche realized the futility of her situation and the siege was ended on the 8 May, when Old Wardour Castle surrendered. The action at Old Wardour Castle, whilst a side show in the war, did prove two things: firstly, it demonstrated just how easily an otherwise minor operation could develop out of all proportion in relation to its tactical importance. Secondly, it showed how the Parliamentarian army had the resources to deploy artillery into action when required.

Old Wardour Castle was rendered untenable and Lady Blanche abandoned the site. Other

Donnington Castle, near Newbury in Berkshire. In 1644 the castle was defended by Royalist forces of 200 men and four pieces of artillery. A Parliamentarian force deployed a massive mortar against the site in 1646, which brought about the surrender of the castle.

The remains of Donnington Castle, slighted after the battle in 1646. Charges of gunpowder were inserted into the walls of the castle, which was then blown up to prevent it being used as a garrison stronghold.

castles across the country would also suffer the effects of artillery bombardment, or even deliberate destruction in an action known as 'slighting'. Those castles variously garrisoned by assorted forces were largely obsolete, dating from an age before gunpowder weapons. Some were sited at strategic points, commanding important road links, but apart from serving as barracks for troops, they had no place in seventeenth-century warfare. Despite this fact, a number were fortified and held for either king or parliament. Size was of no importance, with large and small sites serving as garrisons, from where troops could deploy on operations.

Following their attack and capture, castles were frequently 'slighted', usually by Parliamentarian forces, but the king's troops also used this technique of destruction, to prevent further military use. Slighting involved placing casks of gunpowder into the buildings of the castle and simply igniting them; the resulting explosion destroyed the walls, thereby leaving the castle unusable by either side. This procedure happened many times during the war, the most notable examples being Donnington Castle in Berkshire, Caerphilly in Wales, Basing House near Basingstoke and, to a lesser degree, Farnham Castle in Surrey.

THE CIVIL WAR SPREADS TO WALES

The effects of the Civil War spread across the country, and fighting broke out in Wales, where there was a great concentration of castles dating back to the fourteenth and fifteenth centuries. These fortifications were seized by the opposing forces, and the sites defended by garrisons of well-armed troops. Pembroke Castle, for example, was reinforced by Parliamentarian troops in response to the Royalist seizure of nearby Tenby and Haverfordwest, moves that were followed up in 1644 when the king's men took Cardigan and Carmarthen, and thereby placed most of the country under their military control.

Fighting continued across Wales, before finally reaching a climax at the Battle of Colby Heath on 1 August 1645, where the Parliamentary army achieved a full victory. This was followed up on 18 September when the Parliamentarians defeated a Royalist force at Montgomery in the largest battle of the Civil War to be fought in Wales. The Parliamentary army maintained its pressure against Royalist

Chepstow Castle in Wales, surrendered to a Parliamentarian force in 1645, despite being defended by a garrison of sixty-four men, and armed with seventeen pieces of artillery.

forces, causing them to fall back into a series of castles. These would develop into siege operations, which included the deployment of artillery. Some of these sieges would become such fiercely contested actions that Oliver Cromwell himself would come to Wales in order to oversee the conduct of operations.

The Fall of Chepstow Castle

In May 1648 Oliver Cromwell arrived in Wales to take charge of operations, and one of his first military actions was to direct a siege against Chepstow Castle, held by Sir Nicholas Kemeys. Cromwell ordered troops, under the command of Colonel Ewer, to attack the castle on 11 May. The opening stages led to the town being taken, but the castle remained resolute.

This was not the first time the castle had been attacked. In October 1645 it had been held for the king by a garrison of sixty-five men, but following a siege, it had surrendered to Parliamentarian forces, and seventeen pieces of artillery were captured. The walls of Chepstow Castle are up to nine feet (3m) thick in places, but Cromwell was determined to capture the site. On 25 May, he ordered heavy artillery to bombard the castle, and breaches were made in the area of the walls near the spot called Marten's Tower. A large number of the garrison made good their escape through this gap, but Sir Nicholas was captured and killed by Colonel Ewer's troops.

The length of time that a castle of the medieval period could withstand a siege during the English Civil War depended on a number of factors, the most obvious of which was its state of preparedness. The garrisons in most, if not all of those castles held in Wales for the king, knew it was only a question of time before they were invested. Both sides in the war knew that gunpowder artillery was a major factor in bringing about an end to a siege. Some castles surrendered after only a few days, others held out for weeks and months; in the most extreme case a very few managed to withstand the siege tactics for years. The Civil War had been engaged and

Laugharne Castle in Wales was subjected to artillery bombardment in October 1644. The week-long siege ended only when the attacking Parliamentarian forces used their artillery to fire at extreme close range.

fighting since 1642, but it was not until 1644 that the war proper came to Wales.

The Battle for Laugharne Castle

In 1644 the Royalists ordered Sir Charles Gerard to the area of Laugharne, which was being held for Parliament, with instructions to capture the castle. He arrived in early June 1644, and so sudden and successful was his campaign that by the end of the month he had also taken the castles at Kidwelly, Carmarthen, Newcastle Emlyn and Cardigan, covering an area of more than thirty miles in radius. To the west of Gerard's centre of operations lay Haverfordwest Castle, which was being successfully blockaded by a Royalist fleet armed with cannon. Gerard succeeded in taking Laugharne Castle, but with news of the king's defeat at the Battle of Marston Moor on 2 July 1644, he was instructed to march back to England with the bulk of his forces. Behind him he left a rearguard force and garrisons to hold the castles he had recently seized. One of these was Laugharne Castle, under the command of Lieutenant Colonel Sir William Russell. Gerard probably realized he was being observed, and it is very likely that he knew his movements of withdrawal were an invitation to the Parliamentarian forces to attack his weakened garrisons.

In October, the Parliamentarian commander Major General Laugharne deemed the time to be right, and moved against the reduced garrison at Laugharne Castle. (It was coincidental that the army commander and the target shared the same name, but there was no family connection between the man and the town with its castle.) Laugharne Castle was invested on the evening of 28 October 1644, with Major General Laugharne's troops taking up their positions on the heights about two miles to the north of the castle, from where they could look down directly on to their target. Major General Laugharne's forces had been reinforced, and his artillery train included a powerful demi-culverin, that had been landed from a ship. The siege started with a bombardment coming from the artillery positions about one mile to the east of the castle. The range was really too long, but the gunners kept firing with the aim of reducing the garrison and their defences. The garrison within the castle were holding on to their position, but they were beginning to suffer casualties as the artillery projectiles found their target.

After firing against the castle for three days, it was realized that, due to the extended range, the guns were not making much impression on the target. Major General Laugharne then ordered his artillery to move to a site known as Fern Hill, to the west of the castle, from where his gunners could fire at the gatehouse. He also ordered 200 musketeers from his force to move into the small town and capture it. The castle was now completely cut off, but the garrison still held on determinedly to their positions. On the evening of the 30 October the Parliamentarians seized the town gate and were able to move their artillery into a position where it could fire directly down the main street and at the castle gatehouse. The bombardment continued over the next two days, until finally on 2 November, Laugharne's troops rushed forwards to capture the outer gate of the castle, at around 11pm.

The fighting continued until about 1am on the morning of the 3 November, when the defenders called for a ceasefire in order to permit terms of surrender to be discussed. Having agreed on acceptable terms, the defenders of Laugharne Castle surrendered at 7am. The garrison of some 200 men marched out and their officers left to join the Royalist garrison at Carmarthen. The action had cost the Parliamentarians only ten killed and about thirty wounded. The defenders had lost thirty-three killed and a large number of wounded. The castle at Laugharne was described by a Parliamentarian as: 'One of the holds from whence our forces and the country received the greatest annoyance.' The castle remains were slighted, and sections of the walls were demolished in order to render it useless to the Royalists. The action was but a relatively minor skirmish in the overall scheme of the war, but it had been a harder-fought action than Old Wardour Castle.

Raglan Castle in Wales was besieged by a Parliamentarian army in 1646. The garrison of the castle was equipped with artillery, but the attackers had the advantage of being guaranteed a re-supply of powder and ammunition.

The Siege of Raglan Castle

Lying on the eastern boundaries of Wales is Raglan Castle, which during the Civil War was a very powerful site, well defended and with a reliable garrison. The defences were solid and strong, and known to have included artillery. It was held for the king by the Marquis Henry Somerset, who was so wealthy that it is said he supported the garrison of the castle with a sum of around £40,000. An account written by the Royalist supporter, Richard Symonds, tells how the estate of the marquis was: 'esteemed 24 Thowsand Pounds per annum'. He relates how in 1645 the garrison of Raglan Castle was around 300 men, all being 'constantly paid'. Furthermore, the marquis is believed to have donated some £1,000,000 to the king's war chest, an incredible sum of money.

Apart from the inherent strength of the castle's walls, the garrison set about to construct forward defensive earthworks and fill large wicker baskets, known as gabions, for the protection of gunners and musketeers. These outer works complemented the water-filled moat that surrounded the great hall or keep, and made the site a formidable target to attack. The defenders could be formed in depth both inside and beyond the boundaries from where their artillery could fire back at the attackers. The order to invest the castle was given to Colonel Thomas Morgan, who complied in June 1646. He was an experienced soldier and commanded his forces well. Even so, he found he could not advance against the castle because of the stout defences.

Within his force Morgan had a captain of engineers, John Hooper, who had constructed a battery from where the Parliamentary artillery was able to fire against the castle walls and destroy several pieces of artillery. Hooper set about instructing his men to dig trenches, known as 'saps', which would allow their artillery to be moved closer to the castle while sheltered from the defenders' musket fire. In early August, Sir Thomas Fairfax, commander-in-chief, arrived at the siege to take stock of the situation. More artillery was being brought on to the site, including a huge mortar nicknamed 'Roaring Meg', transported to the siege by Colonel John Birch, governor of Hereford. By now Hooper's trenches were only sixty yards from the walls of the castle. The standard weapons in the siege train of the Parliamentarians' artillery force, such as culverins, would have had a telling impact at such close quarters, but the mortars were undoubtedly more useful in such close proximity to the walls of the castle.

Mortars were used to fire hollow projectiles known as shells; each one was filled with gunpowder and fitted with a rudimentary fuse to detonate it with an explosive force. The barrels of mortars were set to fire their projectiles at very high angles of trajectory in order to shoot them over the walls in a lobbing action. They were short-range weapons, hence the reason for the trenches moving so close to the walls of Raglan Castle. When firing a mortar, timing was essential, and the fuse of the shell had to be lit just before it was sent off. An experienced gunner serving a mortar could calculate with some degree of precision the optimum moment when he had to light the fuse and exactly what its length should be for burning.

Mortar shells, being filled with gunpowder, were designed to explode, causing a great deal of damage to the surrounding target area and killing and wounding troops. A normal solid iron cannon ball, on the other hand, caused only localized damage when it smashed walls, which could be repaired. The blast from a mortar shell when it exploded could also cause fires. Therefore, in the face of such a formidable artillery train, the marquis realized he had no other option but to surrender. His resolve was reaffirmed on 14 August when new trenches were identified as they approached the walls of the castles.

It was suggested that a formal surrender should take place on 19 August. On the agreed day and at the appointed time, the marquis

Raglan Castle in Wales was battered by a strong artillery force, including a powerful mortar called 'Roaring Meg'. When the garrison surrendered in 1646 they were permitted to march out with full 'honours of war', but were required to surrender their artillery.

awaited the arrival of the Parliamentary delegation in the great hall of the castle, the walls of which had been badly battered by artillery, that he '...could see through the window the General (Fairfax) with all his officers entering the Outward Court, as if a floodgate had been left open'.

When the Parliamentarian forces entered Raglan Castle they found much in the way of munitions and twenty pieces of artillery of varying size, but only one barrel of gunpowder. Given the lack of this essential supply for musketeers and artillery, the Parliamentary forces were puzzled as to how the defenders had been able to keep firing their weapons for such a long time. As they searched the castle further they discovered the answer to their question. With great ingenuity and resource the garrison had built a gunpowder mill with which it had been possible to make at least one barrel of gunpowder per day. Given their limited supplies this was a truly remarkable feat. The preparations made by the garrison prior to the siege had been so complete that they had been able to cast their own cannon balls and musket balls.

The method of approach employed at the siege of Raglan Castle to advance the artillery was actually standardized practice. It had originated in Europe and its methods had proved so successful that its use soon spread. It was a relatively straightforward tactic, if somewhat labour-intensive: first, a parallel trench was dug

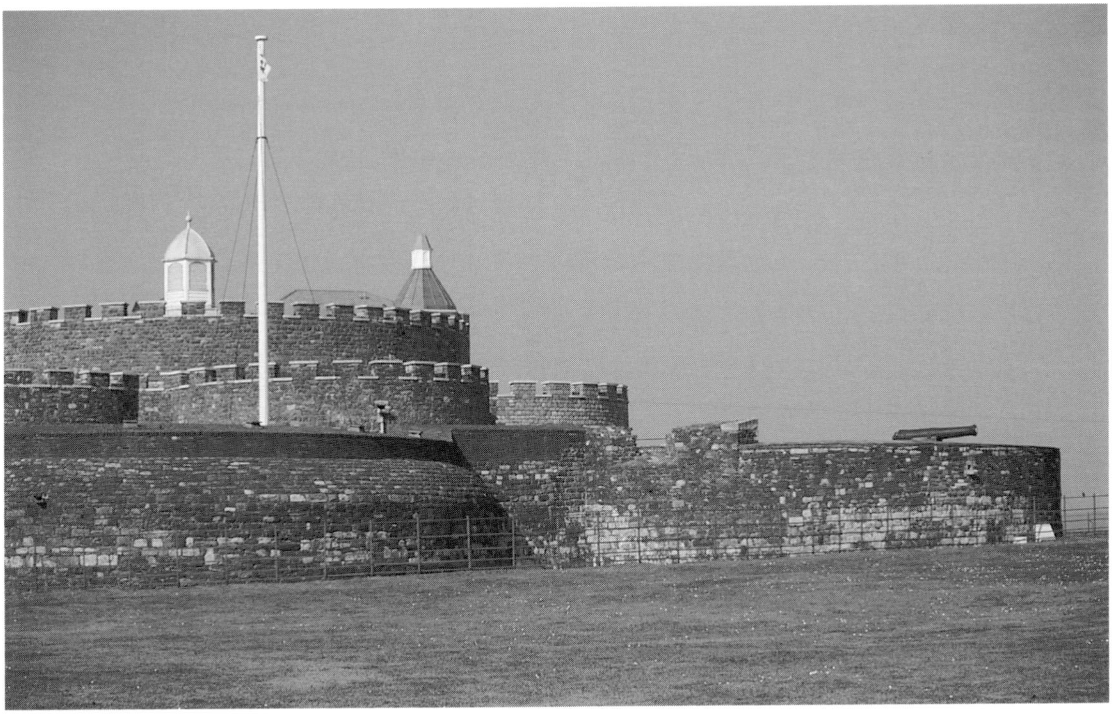

Deal Castle in Kent showing the tiers of gun platforms typical of specialized artillery forts such as this. It was besieged by a force of Parliamentarians in 1648 and surrendered, even though it had been re-supplied by sea.

some 600 to 700yd (550 to 640m) out from the fortification under siege, and very often completely encircled the castle being attacked. From this trench, which was just out of effective reach from the defenders' artillery fire, a number of points would be selected from where an assault or several assaults were to be made. The engineers then dug a series of 'saps' leading towards the target. They used a 'zig-zag' method of approach in order to prevent the defenders from firing down the length of the trench, which could have caused casualties. As the men dug they threw the spoil from the workings up to form earthworks to add height to the parapets for the added protection of the troops.

The distance advanced was usually dictated by the maximum effective range of the artillery of both defenders and attackers; this was usually set at about 300yd (270m). Under good directions engineers might press a sap forward at the rate of about 146yd (134m) in twenty-four hours. At that point a second parallel of trench works would be dug, with additional earthworks being thrown up in front of it to serve as protection for siege-artillery emplacements which were being brought forward by the gunners. Under cover of fire from these guns the labouring engineers would continue the approach and dig further 'saps' towards the target. All the time the siege guns would be firing against the ramparts in an effort to force the defenders to take cover from the attackers' artillery. This was designed to reduce the effects of the defenders' artillery.

Pembroke Castle in Wales was besieged by Parliamentarian forces under the personal direction of Oliver Cromwell, who deployed artillery during the action.

If a breach was made in the wall at this point the attackers could assault and storm the positions. However, there was always the possibility that the defenders might rally and counterattack and force the attackers to withdraw. This happened at Pembroke Castle when Cromwell's men rushed to the breach in the town walls. Should the defenders continue to resist, then a third parallel would have to be dug and more artillery brought up to fire at them. The type of artillery pieces at this stage could also include mortars, which would be used to lob bombs at high angles inside the defences. More often than not it took no more than two days' bombardment from this third parallel to sufficiently silence the defenders' resolve. The marquis at Raglan was probably aware of this, and obviously in a move to save the lives of his men, he elected to surrender the castle.

Troubles at Pembroke Castle

The disbanding of any garrison is never a straightforward matter, and the body of Parliamentarians at Pembroke Castle was aggrieved over lack of payment, and promises that had been reneged on by army councils. The commander of the garrison at Pembroke Castle during the war, John Poyer, demanded due recompense for services rendered by himself and his men, and when this restitution

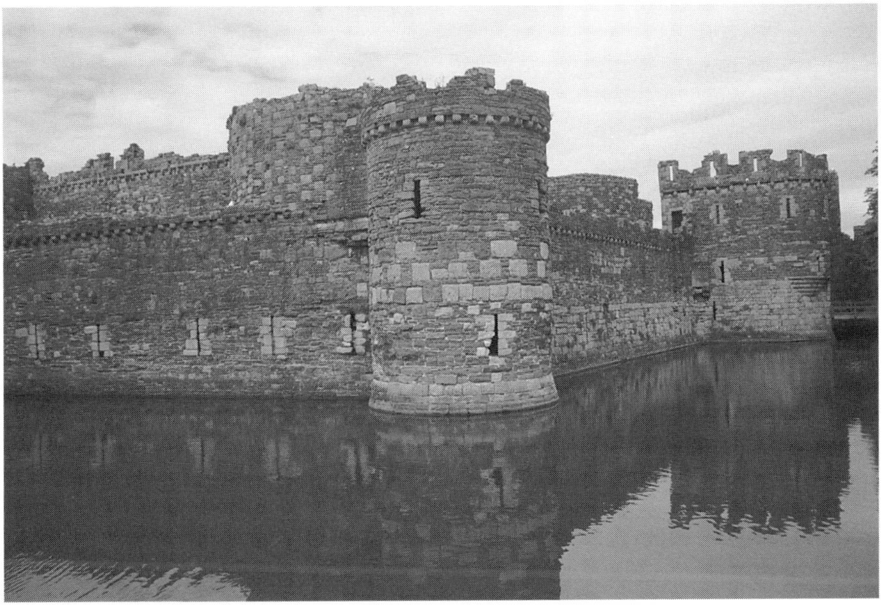

Beaumaris Castle on Anglesey in north Wales was attacked during the Civil War, being captured in October 1648 by a Parliamentarian force of 1,500 men. Its loss meant that the Royalist army had been deprived of another stronghold.

was not forthcoming, he stayed firmly in charge of the immensely strong castle and the walled town. This state of affairs lasted until 1648, when Poyer, for some inexplicable and unexpected reason, decided to declare his allegiance to King Charles. This was betrayal of the highest order, and something that Parliament would not tolerate.

In an effort to resolve the matter, Oliver Cromwell, as Lieutenant General of the Parliamentary army, ordered Colonel Fleming to take over as constable of Pembroke. But as he approached he was attacked and driven off by Colonel Powell, an officer who had remained with John Poyer and the remainder of the garrison. The spirited attack not only drove Fleming out of the town, it also succeeded in capturing two pieces of artillery. Not one to give up his duty, Fleming returned in April and attacked Pembroke; but in the course of this altercation he was killed.

Around this time Major General Rowland Laugharne arrived unexpectedly from London, where he had been under arrest on suspicion of being involved in a Royalist plot. Suspicion turned to conclusive evidence when he joined forces with Colonel Powell, and between them they raised a force of some 8,000 men with Royalist sympathies. They moved on St Fagans, and on 8 May 1648 appeared to be on the verge of gaining a victory against local Parliamentary forces, when a force of Dragoons, commanded by Colonel John Okey, and other troops of the New Model Army, attacked to drive them back.

This act of betrayal prompted Oliver Cromwell to travel to Pembroke to take personal command of operations. He arrived late in May, direct from his siege at Chepstow Castle, and leading a force of some 6,000 men. Immediately he set about investing the town and castle, and positioned his forces so as to prevent the garrison escaping or any relief force arriving. His artillery train was well equipped, and included several naval cannons brought ashore especially for the operation. Cromwell continued to make his preparations for the remainder of May, during which time there were minor skirmishes between the two sides. Cromwell also dealt with the town of Tenby in the same month, the Parliamentarian garrison having changed sides to support the Royalist cause when their commander, Colonel Rice Powell, was absent. It did not take Cromwell long to reduce the town walls with his artillery train, and then the garrison was dealt with; he also captured twenty further cannon that he was able to put to good use at other sieges, as the warring came to an end in Wales.

Meanwhile at Pembroke, the river approach to the castle was blockaded, and the town and site was completely surrounded on all sides by batteries of artillery and infantry. The besiegers succeeded in setting fire to a number of buildings, and managed to blast a breech in the town walls. Despite this, the defenders held out and engaged Cromwell's men in fierce street fighting as the latter attempted to enter the town through the breech in the walls between 15 and 16 June. All the while the besiegers were growing stronger, as more and more reinforcements continued to arrive and join Cromwell's forces.

On 1 July the heavy siege guns of Cromwell's artillery opened their bombardment. Even then the outcome was still far from being decisive, and the defenders appeared to be just as determined to hold out against Cromwell's forces. Exactly what they thought they might achieve against such overwhelming odds is not known, although they probably realized that theirs was a forlorn hope. In the end, the traitors were betrayed when someone from within the garrison informed the besiegers where the source of the defenders' drinking water was, and this valuable resource was immediately cut off.

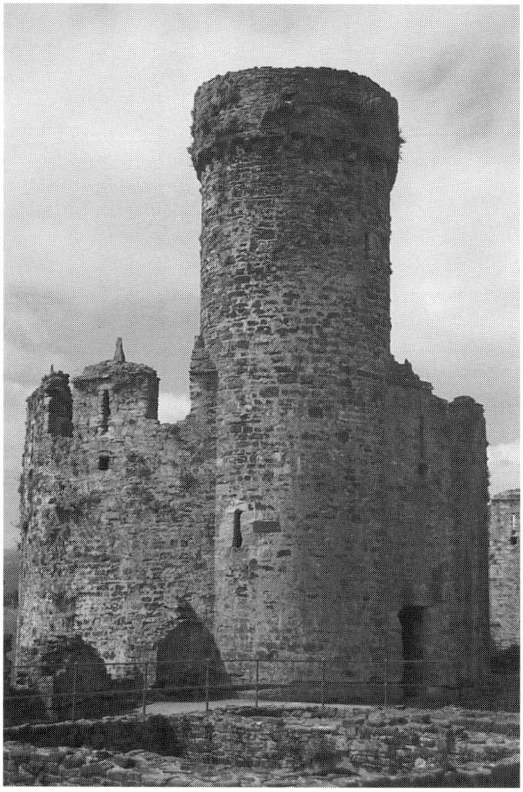

Conwy Castle in North Wales, attacked by a Parliamentarian force in August 1646, which included batteries of artillery. The guns had little effect on the defences, and the castle did not fall until November that year.

Isolated from any would-be Royalist reinforcements and without water, the defenders of Pembroke grew weaker by the day. Left with no option, the three commanding figures – Poyer, Powell and Laugharne – sued for peace and terms of surrender. The garrison was allowed to disperse, but the three leaders were arrested and taken to London, where they were condemned to death by Parliament. In an unusual move the three convicted ringleaders were allowed to draw 'lots' as to who would be executed and who would have their sentences commuted. So they drew lots, and John Poyer lost, and was shot by firing squad in Covent Garden.

It had taken Cromwell seven weeks to subdue Pembroke. The slighting of the castle and town walls was inevitable, and Cromwell gave the following orders: 'Demolish (Pembroke) castle, so as that (it) may not be possest by the enemy.' In fulfilling this order, troops placed charges of gunpowder in the towers of the castle and blasted out sections of the walls.

At the beginning of the Civil War artillery had hardly been afforded a second thought, and it was the dashing élan of the cavalry that attracted attention. But with the establishment of the New Model Army and a review of the artillery train, by the end of the war guns were being used with daring and boldness, a situation that reflected the virtual monopoly held by the Parliamentarians regarding artillery.

THE CIVIL WAR IN THE CHANNEL ISLANDS

The English Civil War was not confined to mainland England and Wales, and fighting also spread to the English possession of the British Channel Islands. Over the years the islands had been fortified, and artillery despatched for their defence; but like the mainland, the islands were divided in their loyalties between king and parliament: Jersey, the largest island in the group declared for the king, while Guernsey, the second largest island, declared for parliament.

The islands had escaped most of the ravages of the fighting, but on 20 October 1651 a Parliamentary force of 3,000 men, commanded by Colonel Heane, landed on Jersey from a fleet of eighty ships in St Ouen's Bay to the west of the island. They marched overland to Mont Orgueil Castle, where Colonel Philip de Carteret surrendered the castle with its artillery force; this included '18 guns and 5 iron "Murderers"'. There is a slight discrepancy concerning the date of surrender, some sources stating it was on 25 October, others that it was two days later, on 27 October. The garrison were not entirely in agreement with their commander's decision, but they had to abide by his orders, and they were permitted to march from the castle with full honours of war. Thus a potential Royalist stronghold had been captured with the minimum of effort. The fact of these landings in the Channel Islands was made possible because the waters around the British Isles were patrolled by ships controlled by Parliament.

The Siege of Elizabeth Castle

The attackers then turned their attention towards the other castle, known as Elizabeth Castle, sited on a rocky promontory in St Aubin's Bay to the south of Jersey, protecting the safe anchorage afforded by the sweep of the bay. Colonel Heane knew this fortification would prove more stubborn. It had strong defences, to which was added the fact that it was cut off from the main island by the sea at high tide. In 1643 sporadic fighting had broken out and the castle was besieged, but without great purpose. The Parliamentarian force realized that with ample supplies, the garrison appeared to be in a strong position, and would try to hold out until relief arrived. But the island was blockaded, and to prove this point the fleet sailed around the coast firing as they went. The fleet is known to have included the Tresco, a frigate with twenty-four guns, and Happy Entrance, a Third Rate with thirty guns.

With their command of the seas, the Parliamentarians were able, between 28 October and 2 November 1651, to transport several batteries of artillery to Jersey for the specific purpose of reducing Elizabeth Castle. The guns were taken ashore where they were to be sited, on the high ground known as Mont de la Ville, or South Hill, from where they had a commanding view across St Aubin's Bay and could fire unimpeded on the castle. The largest battery was formed by six guns firing projectiles of 36lb (16kg) in weight. Mortars were also brought into position, the largest of which, according to the chronicler Jean Chevalier, fired a projectile weighing 450lb (204kg) with an explosive filling of up to 40lb (18kg). Another mortar fired projectiles of 250lb (113kg), with an explosive filling of 25lb (11kg), while a third mortar fired shells of 36lb (16kg) containing 12lb (5.4kg) of explosive. Each of these mortars is recorded as being supplied with 300 projectiles, which, according to the calculations of the late Brigadier General W. Evans, CMG, DSO, Secretary of the Royal Artillery Institution, had calibres of 18.75in (48cm), 14.75in (37cm) and 4.25in 10.7cm respectively. Over a twelve-day period, between 5–17 November, it is believed some thirty-eight mortar projectiles fell directly within the walls of Elizabeth Castle or in close proximity, in addition to which there would have been ordinary artillery fire.

The range and elevation from which these guns were bombarding the castle rendered them safe from return fire, and they could conduct themselves with impunity as they loaded and fired the guns and mortars. The bombardment continued almost unabated until on the night of either 9 or 10 November, a shell landed on the old Abbey Church within the castle and destroyed the building which was being used to store supplies. With its destruction the defenders lost twelve barrels of powder and great quantities of other supplies. The single shell killed sixteen men and wounded a further ten. The batteries continued to fire until 5 December, when the commander of the garrison, Sir George Carteret, surrendered his position.

Goodrich Castle in Hereford, slighted by a Parliamentarian force using artillery after the castle had surrendered in 1646.

The action had been one-sided all along, and the defenders probably knew that it was a foregone conclusion, and that they would ultimately be forced to concede. There are some who would argue that the castle could have been starved into submission, and that is perfectly correct. However, by employing such force to reduce an otherwise insignificant stronghold the Parliamentarians were making a statement. By bringing together such a force of artillery they were declaring that they had the means within their power to face all comers. Writing an analysis of the action in 1685, the Jurat, Philip Dumaresq, estimated that around 500 projectiles of all types were fired at Elizabeth Castle during the entire siege, which lasted fifty days.

Castle Cornet Surrenders

On the island of Guernsey, which had declared support for Parliament, the situation was reversed. Here the last great fortification, Castle Cornet, which had been held by a Royalist garrison for eight years and nine months, finally surrendered on 15 December 1651, making the final act in the 'Third Civil War'.

THE END OF WAR AND ITS AFTERMATH

Charles Stuart and other Royalist supporters had fled into exile in October 1651, from which they were not to return until 1660. Parliament and Cromwell had won the Civil War using the combined tactics of musketeers, cavalry and artillery, and the country was now declared a 'Commonwealth'. It was an uneasy peace, and when Cromwell died on 3 September 1658, there was no one single man with sufficient resourcefulness to hold the country together. A group of Parliamentarian commanders, including General George Monck, formed an alliance that would lead to the restoration of the royal family.

In 1660, King Charles II came to the English throne. Little thought was being given to either the army or artillery, which was still being stored in various locations, including the Tower of London, and corruption was leading to a breakdown in authority within the military. The men in charge of this were really only custodians. Records from 1661 show that the army strength was 40,000, and from amongst these there were only forty-eight master gunners. A reorganization programme was instituted, and by 1663 the standing army had been reduced to 3,574 men in regiments. As regulation returned, the military grew in size and ability, and by 1667 the militia numbered 12,000 infantry and 3,200 cavalry. The artillery was also reorganized, and in 1670 there were 103 men holding posts as paid gunners, and further training was promised for other gunners.

The fact that England kept its artillery, stocks of gunpowder and ammunition in the Tower of London – which, after all, is a fortress – was nothing unusual. A number of European countries were also keeping their most important artillery force in well guarded, centralized locations, that served as arsenals. In France, for example, this was the Bastille, and in Russia it was the Kremlin, both of which were also fortresses and symbols of state strength.

8 Barrel Casting

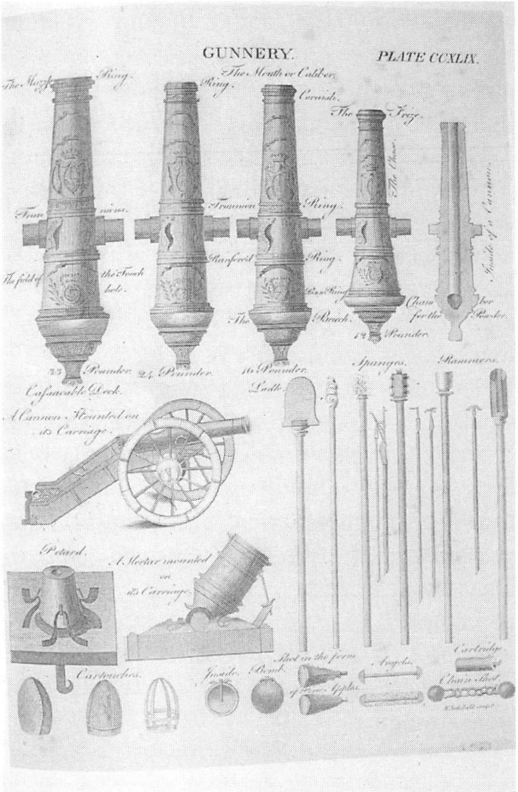

Various types of barrels and tools, including swabs and rammers, used in association with the loading and firing of artillery during the seventeenth century.

The barrel is undoubtedly the most significant part of any piece of artillery, no matter what the calibre. It is the size of bore or tube of the barrel that determines the weight and size of a projectile, and thus governs the destructiveness of the ammunition. It could be argued that the barrel is simply the means of delivery, because it determines the range through elevation and weight of gunpowder charge, and when fired sets the projectile on its trajectory towards the target. But there is much more to it than just that: the barrel not only makes the weapon readily identifiable, it is what makes the weapon, because without it the projectile could not be fired.

In the seventeenth century, casting still remained the main method of producing barrels for artillery. In fact casting was the most cost-effective means of producing barrels for all types of weapon, including mortars and guns of varying calibres. Unfortunately, the techniques employed in the process had not progressed that much from those used in the sixteenth century, and the process still involved pouring huge volumes of molten metal into a mould of the correct shape and size. In order to cast a barrel for a weapon capable of firing a projectile weighing 40lb (18kg), some 5,600lb (2,540kg) of iron (2.5 tons) had to be poured into the mould. This figure provides some idea of how much metal was being absorbed just to produce artillery. The weight of metal involved in the process would be proportionally greater or less, depending on the calibre of barrel being cast.

Preparing moulds for the casting of cannon barrels in the late seventeenth century.

AN INCREASING DEMAND

In coping with the huge amounts of metal being used, the skills of the men working in the foundries inevitably developed through experience, and over the years their levels of competence to handle such increased capacities of molten metal greatly improved. The furnaces became hotter and more efficient, the crucibles to transfer the molten metal to the moulds were larger, and the foundries increased in size and became specialized. As demand for artillery increased, pressure to produce more was placed on the foundries. But casting was a process that could not be rushed: the molten metal had to be readied and poured into the mould as a single transference, after which it had to be allowed to cool and harden – and all this took time.

In an effort to meet these demands, those countries with the capability to produce their own artillery expanded their established armaments' centres even further. They also established more production centres around the country. In Russia, for example, cannon foundries were established outside the important city of Moscow. To give some idea of the increase in demand for artillery, gun founders in France were ordered to produce 400 new weapons of varying calibre, to permit the reorganization of the country's artillery force under the direction of Maximilian de Bethune, Duc de Sully. In addition to artillery for armies, there were also the expanding naval forces to be equipped. This reaction was happening all across Europe and into the Far East, where nations were coming into conflict over trade and territory.

The new gun foundries were being established in areas where there were natural deposits of the raw materials, such as iron and copper, that were required for casting barrels. A nearby source of fuel, such as coal or wood, that could be turned into charcoal for the furnaces was

Work in a gun foundry, with moulds being prepared by labourers in readiness to cast barrels for cannons.

also deemed beneficial – though not essential because this could be transported to the site as necessary. The practice was innovative, but not entirely new. During the reign of King Henry VIII, 1509 to 1547, gun foundries had been established in south-east England around the area of Weald in Sussex, where all these factors were recognized as being essential for the continued production of artillery. In the seventeenth century these foundries were still in operation, and producing cast barrels for a range of weapons.

MANUFACTURING COSTS

As the demand for weapons increased, so too did the price of raw materials. During the sixteenth century iron guns had cost in the order of £10 per ton, and by the seventeenth century this figure had increased to £13 per ton. Iron guns were always less expensive than those weapons with barrels made from bronze, but they were also less popular with the gunners who had to contend with the weight. During the period of the Commonwealth in England, Oliver Cromwell favoured iron guns, probably because they were less expensive and therefore more could be purchased. Pieces of cast-iron artillery known as 'culverin drakes' were being cast for

Conditions in a typical gun foundry of the seventeenth century: melting metal, pouring and stoking the furnaces.

Cromwell in 1652 by gun-founders such as Thomas Ffoley and George Brown. The weight of a typical 5.5in- (14cm-) calibre culverin-drake was in the order of 2,000lb (907kg), which meant that such weapons would have cost less than £12.

Bronze was undoubtedly more reliable, but it was ten times more expensive than cast-iron guns, and this meant that some military commanders preferred quantity to quality. Cast iron was brittle, and a side effect of casting was that air bubbles formed as the molten metal cooled down, both factors that could lead to weaknesses in the cast barrel. Bronze did not produce any such side effects, and had a better elastic reaction to the high pressure in the powder chamber when the weapon was fired. When a cast-iron barrel failed on firing it did so without any warning and with destructive consequences, killing all the crew. A bronze barrel, on the other hand, showed signs of beginning to weaken, the most obvious being that the barrel, particularly around the powder chamber, began to swell; this indicated that the pressure on firing was weakening the barrel. It would then be taken out of service before an accident happened. Despite this, cast iron continued to be used, although as the seventeenth century progressed the trend favoured the more reliable range of bronze weapons.

View along the bronze barrel of a late seventeenth-century gun. This shows the thickened breech area where the propellant charge was ignited to fire the gun.

CASTING METHODS

Barrels were being cast using two methods, each of which allowed either cast iron or bronze to be used in the manufacturing process. The first and older form of casting produced a hollow barrel formed around a central mandrel to produce the bore. This method was tried and tested, but it was not without its defects. As early as the sixteenth century Niccolo Targalia, generally recognized as being the father of ballistics, noted that the central mandrel sometimes moved during the casting process and thus affected the true line of the bore. The inner surface of the barrel was also far from being smooth, because air bubbles produced pitting or slight bumps.

Targalia realized that these defects would affect the accuracy of the weapon. He knew that the projectiles were slightly smaller than the diameter of the bore, and as a consequence some of the force from the propelling charge

A French field gun made from bronze, showing the embellishments being added to the barrel to identify ownership and details of the size of the projectile. This shows the touch hole, the 'cap squares' to secure the trunnions to the carriage, and the lifting handles referred to as 'dolphins'.

of gunpowder passed around the projectile on being fired. The projectile would also strike these defects and cause inaccuracy. Targalia noted that if a projectile struck a slight rise on the right-hand side of the barrel before it emerged from the muzzle, the ball would deviate to the right; gunners therefore had to be made aware of this, and a remedy devised.

Reaming out the Barrel

The solution was to ream out the barrel with a boring machine. This type of equipment had been used in woodworking for some time, but its application to metalworking was innovative. The first boring machines to be used in this fashion were fitted with long shafts tipped with iron cutting bits to smooth out the defects and clean the bore. Leonardo da Vinci is one of the figures who can lay claim to devising this principle, and some of his drawings show such devices intended for the purpose of smoothing the bore of barrels. The other claimant is Vannoccio Vincenzio Austino Luca Biringuccio, a metal founder from Sienna in Italy. In his work *Pirotechnia*, published in 1558, Biringuccio illustrated how a horizontally mounted boring machine, operated by waterpower, could be used to smooth defects inside barrels for artillery of all calibres. The barrel was advanced on to the cutting and smoothing tool by levering it forwards.

It is open to debate as to who originally devised the idea, but the process certainly went on to revolutionize barrel manufacture. In the seventeenth century the boring process would be taken to the next stage and the method further improved.

Producing a Solid Casting

The second method of manufacturing barrels for artillery involved the metal being poured into the mould to produce a solid casting. The first stage in this process was to make an exact replica, or pattern, of the gun. The full-size model was built up starting by tightly winding stout rope on to a wooden core. Around this a team of workmen carefully layered clay to produce the shape of the barrel. Once the clay

Applying the finish to moulds being readied for casting barrels for cannons. This type of work was being repeated all across Europe.

A boring machine of the seventeenth century. It would appear to be a finishing process also, as small protuberances would need to be removed and the interior of the barrel smoothed to permit easy loading.

had dried on this positive model, a coating of wax was applied. Then an outer layer of clay was added and allowed to harden. The layer of wax prevented the clay from adhering to the model, which could then be re-used to make further moulds, thereby speeding up the manufacturing process. The outer crust was removed in two halves to produce a negative imprint of the gun inside the clay casing. The two pieces of the mould were fitted together and held in place by iron bands. The mould was placed upright in a casting pit in front of the furnace; it was well supported to take the extra weight as the molten metal was poured in a single casting.

The casting was allowed to cool and solidify, after which the mould was removed from the casting pit and the outer clay was broken away from the casting. If all looked well and the gunsmiths were satisfied, the barrel was taken to another part of the foundry where it was bored using the new technique, and converted into a gun. The positive model, meanwhile, would again be coated in wax and made ready for the process once more. This method of production greatly speeded up output. The new boring techniques were advocated by gunsmiths such as the Verbruggen family from Holland. The old method of boring had been transformed by moving the cutting tools from a horizontal to a vertical plane. The solid cast barrel was then suspended in a frame and attached to pulleys and winches, where the weight of the barrel was sufficient to lower it on to the cutting or boring tools which were operated by waterpower.

By casting the barrel as a solid piece, the problems of weaknesses such as tiny fractures and air bubbles were eliminated. The frame to which the barrel was attached for boring was set square, and the cutting tools produced a much truer bore, giving better accuracy and reliability. After boring, the touch-hole or vent would then be drilled, and after proofing, the barrel was ready to enter service. The process was cost-effective in many ways, because not only was production improved, but the workers functioned much better, and the metal that was bored out could be returned to the furnace for re-use on further barrels.

The same casting technique, using disposable negative clay moulds cast from a standard positive mould, also improved the production of iron cannon balls; this led to a standardization of calibres, and improved overall performance. Before, vibration of the barrel caused by an ill-fitting projectile seriously compromised accuracy, already notoriously bad, the problem arising as the projectile moved along the barrel during firing. Improved casting for cannon balls redressed this problem. In 1627 Sir Thomas Smith produced a work entitled *Art of Gunnery*, in which he describes how a vibration on firing could affect weapon performance and cause the projectile to veer away from its true course, either through a badly cast barrel or cannon ball. The phenomenon of vibration was well known, and gunners knew that a properly cast barrel would have no such defect and therefore be more accurate. To prove his observations, Sir Thomas punished a soldier who had committed an infraction by sentencing him to sit astride the barrel of a piece of artillery whilst it was fired. The result of the experiment is recorded:

> I asked the opinion of a soldier, who for a trespass committed was enjoined to ride the cannon, who confidently affirmed, he could perceive no quivering of the metal of the piece, but that the air which issued out of the mouth and touch-hole of the piece did somewhat astonish and shake him.

It is quite probable that the barrel may have been a mechanically bored piece, which was very fortunate for the convicted man.

Multi-Barrelled Cannons

Some weapon designers of artillery did not see why weapons necessarily had to be of single chamber, and during the seventeenth century there was a brief return to try and develop multi-barrelled cannons. One of these designers was Antonio Petrini, who invented double-barrelled cannon, with the tubes joined together at an angle of 30 degrees. It was intended that the design fired the two barrels simultaneously to discharge a pair of cannon balls linked by a length of chain.

The idea was similar in approach to the multi-barrelled designs created by the gunfounder Peter Baude, who worked for Henry VIII at Houndsditch in London between 1528 and 1546. One of the most famous of these designs was a triple-barrelled, breech-loaded weapon with a calibre of 2.12in (5.38cm), though on this weapon, each barrel fired independently of the others. Petrini claimed that his gun could produce ‘the greatest destruction’, and in theory it would have wreaked havoc against the rigging of ships and caused deadly injuries to gunners – but trying to time the discharge of two at the same instant was impossible. Even if the charge of the gunpowder propellant was equal in both barrels, and even allowing for the fact that the gunners could have fired the weapon in unison, there would have been a momentary delay in firing, and this slight but marginal difference in discharging

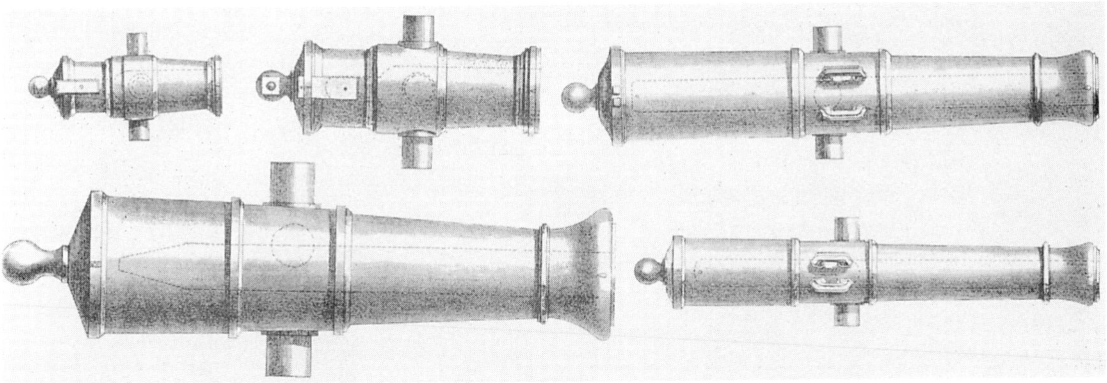

Range of various types of artillery barrel cast during the seventeenth century. Detail of the chamber is shown where the powder would be rammed, and the contrast between the reduced chamber and a straight barrel can be clearly seen. All have trunnions, but only the two barrels on the right have 'dolphins' or lifting handles as part of the casting.

the barrels would have caused the weapon to rip itself apart. This was realized by people with more experience than Petrini, and needless to say the weapon never entered service.

THE GUN CARRIAGE: DESIGN AND MANUFACTURE

Gun carriages for the artillery were being built under the direction of master carpenters, who oversaw the manufacture in either government workshops or those of a private contractor. This was true in England, and the practice extended to other countries, where the master carpenter was held accountable for the building of gun carriages. Gun carriages by this time were almost universally fitted with two wheels connected, and sides, often referred to as 'cheeks', in which there were recesses to accept the trunnions and thereby support the barrel. The trunnions were secured in place by metal brackets called 'capsquares' that fitted over the top of the trunnions and were bolted to the frame of the carriage. This simple fitting prevented the barrel from being jolted off the carriage when it was moved at speed over rough terrain, but still permitted elevation. This was in common with artillery mounted on ships, but exactly who devised the principle of the capsquare, or where it originated, is not entirely clear.

Part of the carriage design for use with artillery on land was known as a trail, and incorporated a pair of shafts forming rearward-facing arms that rested on the ground and partly supported the weight of the gun. The trail also served as a rudimentary shock absorber when the gun carriage rolled back on its wheels under the recoil force during firing. The trail had fittings to which the transport horses could be harnessed, or ropes attached for hauling by the gunners themselves.

PROOFING THE BARREL

Proofing the barrels of artillery was just as important in the seventeenth century as it was in earlier days. The strength of the barrels had to be established through test firings using charges of gunpowder generally in excess of those normally used on a particular design. Before actual proofing took place it was often

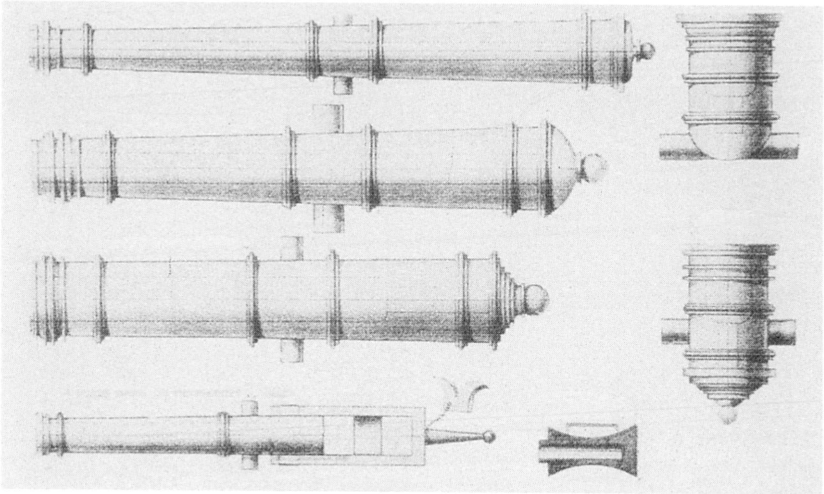

Various types of artillery, ranging from the petrieroes or 'stone thrower' (bottom left) to the trabuccho (top right), a type of mortar, an example of which is directly beneath it.

customary for several men working in the foundry to pound on the completed barrel with heavy hammers: this would detect any defects such as fine cracks, which would produce a distinct tell-tale noise. If such weaknesses were found, then the barrel would be rejected and consigned to the furnace for re-melting and recasting. Each country had its own area where such testing was completed, and sometimes the weapons were accidentally tested to destruction with attendant loss of life among those conducting the proofing.

In England between 1665 and 1680 the proof of ordnance was moved from Moorfields to the naval depot at Woolwich, where a proof-master and 'His Majesty's Founder of Brass and Iron Ordnance' supervised the construction of ordnance and advised on matters concerning manufacture of all ordnance for His Majesty's naval and military forces. In August 1688 records from this proof area tell us that two gunners were buried, presumably when the weapon exploded during testing. Damage is also recorded to houses in the area from around that time, with compensation being made for damage to dwellings affected by the proof firing. The metal from failed gun barrels would not be wasted, being returned to the furnaces for recycling in further castings.

At one time during this period the famous diarist Samuel Pepys held the appointment of Clerk of Acts on the Navy Board, and as such was required to watch artillery being proof-fired; he recorded details of his visits to such locations as the Old Artillery Ground, near Spitalfields. On 20 April 1669 he was due to watch the testing of a new weapon referred to in his observations 'which from the shortness and bigness they do call Punchinello'. Unfortunately he arrived too late to watch the proceedings, but a description of the gun tells us how it was tested against a weapon with twice the barrel length of Punchinello and loaded with a powder charge twice the weight. It appears that Punchinello proved more accurate and was easier to handle than the larger weapon.

It has been opined that Punchinello may have been the forerunner of a weapon design called a 'carronade', which would not enter naval service until the eighteenth century. It seems unlikely, however, that a gun foundry would go to all the bother and expense of building a prototype and not have it enter service. The carronade would not be developed and

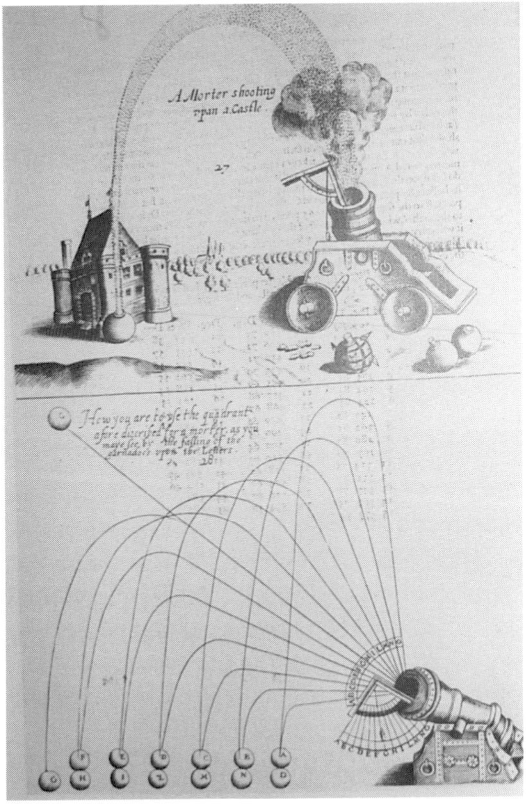

Mortars firing with their barrel set at high and a low angle of trajectory. This shows the parabolic arc of the mortar projectile or bomb as it fired and achieves its plunging effect towards the target.

A French field gun showing the stout construction of the carriage and the large wheels to improve mobility. The trail rests on the ground and would be fitted with ropes to allow the weapon to be towed by either men or horses. Later this would be equipped with 'limber' wheels to give greater manoeuvrability.

enter service with the Royal Navy until 1778, so one has to conclude that what Samuel Pepys recorded may have actually been a mortar, which was in use on 'bomb ketches' at the time.

INTO THE NINETEENTH CENTURY

Barrel-casting techniques were greatly improved, but manufacturing output was far from being mass production. Admittedly production was increased, but it would be at least another 150 years before mass production was even being considered. All weapons were now muzzle-loaded, and this method, too, would remain the main loading principle until the late nineteenth century. There were some old-fashioned breech-loading types dating back from earlier periods, but as armies modernized their artillery branch, these outmoded weapons were replaced. The fanciful names were dropped as terms to identify weapons, and instead the weight of the projectile was used to specify the piece of artillery.

9 Naval Artillery

English warships of the seventeenth century were well built and mounted a variety of weaponry.

By the seventeenth century warship design had come a long way, and vessels were developing into seaworthy platforms on which artillery could be mounted properly; increasingly they were driven by sail, and all but a few of the old-fashioned galleys powered manually by banks of oars would finally disappear in this period. This meant that the ship sides were now clear, and cannons could be mounted on gun decks and fired through special openings in the ship's side called 'gun ports'. By this time artillery had been regularly deployed in ships for some 150 years; thus in 1345 the *Christopher* of King Edward III of England had mounted several guns, and weapon designs for specific use on warships were also being developed and introduced into service. One range of this improved weaponry was known as 'drakes', with versions being referred to as 'culverin drakes', and weighing 2,000lb (907kg). Made from cast iron, these weapons were being cast at English gun foundries such as that operated by Thomas Ffoley and George Brown around 1652, at a time when the country was governed by Oliver Cromwell in a period referred to as 'the Commonwealth', because King Charles had been executed in 1649.

THE DRAKE RANGE OF IMPROVED WEAPONRY

The term 'drake' (sometimes known as 'dragon') is believed to have originated back in the late sixteenth century during the reign of Queen Elizabeth Tudor. At that time records tell us that weapons in the drake range included the 'demi-cannon drake' weighing 3,000lb (1,360kg), and the 'demi-culverin drake' and 'saker drake' weighing 1,500lb (680kg) and 1,200lb (544kg) respectively.

The term 'drake' is thought to be a technical reference to describe the interior design of the gun barrel, which narrows down at the breech to form a reduced powder chamber instead of following an even cylindrical bore all the way down. This produced 'shoulders' on which the ball rested instead of only being separated from the powder charge by the wadding. The drake design produced a lighter weapon that was better suited for use at sea, but it could be used on land, and indeed was pressed into such service when the need arose. In fact an extra lightweight version weighing only 250lb (113kg), which could be pulled by one horse, was introduced for a short period. The drake was a muzzle-loaded piece of artillery, and in naval use the barrel was shorter than the version used on land, in order to make it easier to load on board a ship.

We know how effective drakes could be when used in land battles, through a number of written observations. The first was made at the Battle of Chester in 1643, during the English Civil War, when a single-round shot from a drake firing a 5lb (2.2kg) ball is recorded as killing sixty men in a unit deployed with King Charles's army. This may seem an unduly large number of casualties from a single shot, but there could be a number of reasons for this. First, being formed in close ranks it is possible that a single ball of that weight could penetrate deeply into the files of men. Second, the troops might have panicked and caused injuries amongst themselves, and these were later attributed to the single shot. Third, and most likely, it was probably an over-exaggeration by the gunners.

At the Battle of Nantwich on 25 January 1644, Sir William Brereton of the Parliamentarian forces opened fire with his drakes using 5lb (2.2lb) balls that 'caused more terror than execution'. The cannon balls impacted on the hard, flinty surface, sending up great shards of stony splinters and causing the Royalists to turn away shouting 'Let us fly, for they have great ordnance!.' This last reference would bear out the possibility of a combination of panic and over-exaggeration from the Chester engagement with drakes. From these references, however, there is no reason to believe that drakes were any less effective when deployed at sea.

In fact we only need look at an inventory of the armament of the formidable warship *Sovereign of the Seas*: with a displacement of 1,600 tons, she was launched in 1637 during the reign of King Charles I of England, and was equipped with a range of drakes to provide firepower. Forming the broadside battery on the gun deck were twenty cannon drakes, with eight demi-cannon drakes as stern and bow chasers. These last two types of weapon were designed to permit the ship to fire at a pursuing enemy vessel, or to fire on a target when giving chase. On the middle deck of the *Sovereign of the Seas* the broadside was made up with twenty-four culverin drakes and six culverin as chase guns. On the upper deck there were twenty-four demi-culverin drakes in broadside, with four demi-culverins as chase guns mounted in the stern. Completing this there were eight demi-culverin drakes on

Shipbuilders in England had learned much, and by the seventeenth century were able to mount artillery in large numbers in warships.

the fo'c'sle, six on the half-deck, and two more on the quarter-deck.

This gives a total of 102 pieces of artillery, although some sources state that the *Sovereign of the Seas* may have had 108 guns. She was designed and built by Master Shipwright Phineas Pett, who in 1610 had built the *Prince Royal*, mounting fifty-six guns. The ship was the pride of King Charles' navy, and rightly so, for she was one of the largest warships anywhere in service at that time. Indeed, it was apparently on the orders of King Charles that the *Sovereign of the Seas* was so heavily armed. But even so, as a gun platform it was nothing compared to the 1,500 ton *Henri Grace à Dieu* that had served in the navy of King Henry VIII and had mounted 250 guns. The difference between these ships was the fact that the *Sovereign of the Seas* had its weaponry spread out over three decks with gun ports so the weapons could be 'run out' or deployed when the enemy approached.

GUN PORTS

Gun ports were a feature believed to have originated in France, and were nothing new to ship design in the seventeenth century, having been used on earlier designs such as the *Mary Rose*, which weighed 700 tons and was designed to carry sixty pieces of artillery including culverins. This magnificent ship was lost in June 1545, when she sailed out to meet an attacking French fleet that was approaching the English south coast just off Spithead. Henry VIII was watching from Southsea castle when the ship began to list and take on water through the gun ports, which were open. The inevitable happened, and the *Mary Rose* sank as Henry and other onlookers watched helplessly. The ship had eighty guns on board, and according to one account, the lower ledges of the gun ports were only 16in (40cm) from the water. The crew of over 400 had been increased by more than 300 soldiers serving as archers and hand-gunners, and it is possible that, with more guns than the design allowed for, and with open gun ports, she was top-heavy, and when she manoeuvred, the water rushed in.

This was not to be the only such loss through open gun ports, because on 10 August 1628, the Swedish warship *Wasa* suffered the same fate as *Mary Rose*: with sixty-four guns, of which forty-eight were mounted on two

Warships of the seventeenth century such as these English designs were seaworthy platforms for artillery.

gun decks, it has been claimed that the *Wasa*, too, was top-heavy, and when she manoeuvred, took on water through the open gun ports. Such features posed a problem in deploying artillery at sea, and new tactics and sailing practices had to take gun ports into account.

A NAVAL ARMS RACE

In the first half of the seventeenth century a naval arms race arose between several European nations in an attempt to see which side could fit the most number of guns into a ship. The Dutch began a building programme that launched ships armed with sixty guns; the Swedish navy responded with the sixty-four-gun *Wasa*, whose twenty-four-pounder cannons had a range of over 700yd (640m); and England was building the *Prince Royal* with fifty-six guns. The *Sovereign of the Seas*, 1,700 tons, continued in service for an incredible fifty years until it was lost in an accidental fire in 1696. Thus the way forward was paved by ships such as these, with their heavy firepower. The effective range to which these weapons could fire was about 250yd (228m), and had a striking power that enabled warships to sink their opponents, rather than just crippling them.

The weight of the firepower unleashed by the weaponry such as was carried on these ships made them truly formidable. The importance of having good gunnery at sea had been recognized as early as 1578, when William Bourne wrote his treatise *The Arte of Shooting in Great Ordnaunce*: ' if you shoote when the other Ship is aloft on top of the Sea, you have a bigger marke… there is no better time for to give fire than when shee is beginning to rise on the Sea'. In this remark Bourne points out the practicalities of firing when the enemy ship is fully exposed and representing the much bigger target.

In 1642, on the outbreak of the English Civil War, Admiral William Batten, who served on Parliament's side, drew up a survey of the fleet that would play an important role in the fighting. The list he drew up is presented in the table on page 114.

By the middle of the seventeenth century warships began to be termed in categories according to the armament they carried. Ships in the English navy, as seen in the table on page 114 for example, were in six categories, and classed as 'rates' according to their weight and the number of guns carried. The method of classification was not a hard and

William Batten's fleet list of 1642

	Tons	*Crew*	*Guns*
First Rate:			
Sovereign	1,522	600	90
Prince	1,187	500	70
Merhonour	946	350	40
Second Rate:			
Defiance	857	250	38
Rainbow	731	240	40
Constant Reformation	742	250	40
Victory	721	260	40
Swiftsure	746	260	46
St Andrew	783	260	42
St George	792	260	44
Triumph	776	300	44
Vanguard	751	250	40
Henrietta Maria	793	250	42
Charles	810	250	44
Unicorn	767	250	46
James	875	250	48
Third Rate:			
Assurance	600	200	34
Dreadnought	552	140	30
Convertine	621	200	34
Antelope	512	160	38
Happy Entrance	539	160	30
Garland (sometimes written as Guardland)	567	170	34
Bonaventure	557	170	32
Swallow	478	150	34
Leopard	515	160	34
Lion	620	170	40
Fourth Rate:			
Mary Rose	321	100	25
Expedition	301	110	14
Providence	304	110	14
Fifth Rate:			
Eighth Whelp	162	60	14
Tenth Whelp	186	60	14

William Batten's fleet list of 1642 *continued*

Sixth Rate:			
Henrietta Maria (a pinnance)	68	25	6
Greyhound	128	50	12
Roebuck	90	45	10
Nicodemus	105	50	6

Type	*Weight of shot*	*Range*
Demi-cannon	32-pounder	340yd
Cannon-perrier	24-pounder	320yd
Culverin	18-pounder	400yd
Demi-culverin	9-pounder	400yd
Saker	5-pounder	340yd

fast rule, but more of a general guidance, as can be seen from Batten's *Fleet Survey*. Thus first-rate ships carried more than ninety guns; second-rate carried between eighty and ninety guns; third-rate had between fifty and eighty guns; fourth-rate ships carried between thirty-eight and fifty guns; fifth-rate had between eighteen and thirty-eight guns; and the sixth-rate ship of the line carried fewer than eighteen guns. We learn from records that by 1684, naval artillery was beginning to be termed according to the weight of shot they fired, rather than being classified by name or weapon type. For example, fourth-rate ships were mounting twelve-pounder culverins on the gun deck, six-pounders on the upper deck and 5.5-pounder sakers on the quarter-deck. The main types of armament carried by ships at this period fell into five main types (see above).

The artillery pieces of larger calibre, provided they were served by a good crew, could fire between ten and twelve shots an hour. The lighter calibres could fire more often, but the crew had to constantly keep in mind that the weapon might overheat and possibly burst.

POOR QUALITY CANNON

With more ships being launched, this in turn led to an increase in demand for artillery. The gun foundries were working at top speed and some compromised the quality of their weapons for quantity. Only two years before the naval arms race, in 1626, Captain John Smith, an English colonist in the American state of Virginia, wrote of poor quality cannon that were: '... honeycombed.... When she is ill cast or overmuch worn she will be rugged within, which is dangerous.... when any rag of her wadding being afire and sticking there, may fire the next charge you put in her.' Poor casting of barrels was widespread, and what John Smith was highlighting in this account was already common knowledge. But by identifying the fact that burning wadding might be stuck inside the barrel after firing, he is pointing out the necessity to sponge out the barrel between shots with a wet swabbing tool. This would prevent accidental ignition during the loading drill, which could have fatal consequences.

The loading drills for guns on board ship were exactly the same as on land, except the fighting area was more confined. The tools used in loading were almost identical, apart from some, such as the rammers and swabbing sponges, that could be fitted with rope instead of wooden handles. This again reflected the lack of space between decks.

A barrel mounted on a wooden carriage typical of the type used on seventeenth-century warships.

The rope handle would be twisted to make it more rigid, yet still allow some degree of flexibility in order to manipulate the rammer to tamper the powder charge and projectile into the chamber.

GUN PRODUCTION AND COSTS

At the end of the sixteenth century and into the beginning of the seventeenth, barrels for artillery, intended for both land and navy service, were being cast in vertical moulds with a central mandrel or core that provided the bore. Bronze was the preferred metal for barrels because it did not corrode in the salty conditions at sea, and also barrels cast from bronze would bulge during firing when they were weak and likely to burst. However, bronze was far more expensive than iron, partly because it was an alloy consisting of copper with at least 10 per cent tin; the best quality came from Germany.

When King Henry VIII closed the monasteries in England, his gun founders had a ready supply of bronze from the bells, which they put to good use for the king, who was establishing a powerful artillery train. There was also a rule of war whereby a victorious army could make a claim against a town or city that had been conquered, seizing spoils; this included what was known as 'the right to the bells', which, being made from large amounts of bronze, could be sold for profit to a gun foundry. Naval guns were now of the muzzle-loaded type, with old breech-loaders being replaced by the newer designs of weapon. In 1626 iron guns were passed for use in the English navy following a report by a commissioner who stated: 'Casting improvements make iron guns equal to, or even superior to bronze guns.' Captain John Smith would have disagreed, but it did lead the way to the development of the lighter drake range of guns for naval service.

With an increase in ship armament, this meant that the crews had to be highly competent gunners as well as seamen. Artillery at sea enabled a nation to keep its sea-lanes open for trade and to protect its merchantmen and commerce. In 1652, England had just finished fighting a very bloody and protracted civil war, and Oliver Cromwell's rule in England as the Lord Protector was absolute. He is known to have preferred ordering iron guns such as the drakes on the grounds of economy, because bronze was such an expensive metal for use in guns: an iron gun cost £13 per ton to produce, whilst a bronze gun cost in excess of £80 per ton. This reasoning in England went against the thinking of European naval planners and tacticians, who preferred bronze or brass guns because they did not rust, unlike the iron weaponry. In general terms, however, except for the weight and the cost, there was not much difference in performance between guns made from brass or those that were cast from iron of a comparable calibre.

THE ENGLISH VERSUS THE DUTCH

Cromwell's generals who went to sea against the Dutch in 1652 as his 'instant admirals' were not natural seamen, and they found naval warfare to be far removed from tactics used on land. Despite this, they led the English navy in a series of victories against the Dutch. By 1653 these army commanders, including General George Monck, were using the tactics as laid out in *Fighting Instructions* and inflicting heavy losses amongst the Dutch navy. For example, on 31 July 1653, George Monck fought a twelve-hour battle against a Dutch force of 100 ships at the Battle of Scheveningen. The Dutch lost thirty ships and 1,600 men; Monck lost fewer than half that number.

Several years later, in 1660, the English monarchy in the person of King Charles II was restored after the death of Oliver Cromwell. In that year, the king found he had a fleet of 154 ships with a combined tonnage of almost 57,500 tons, and bestowed on the force the title of Royal Navy. Later he would come up against the same problem concerning lack of naval commanders as faced by Cromwell when King Charles sent commanders of Royalist armies to sea against the Dutch in 1665. By using the reference work *Fighting Instructions* the king's naval commanders would keep the Dutch in check.

Between 1652 and 1673, England fought three naval wars with the Dutch, who were a natural seafaring nation. The Dutch fought commendable actions, and on occasion even defeated the English; they were therefore able to hold their own, along with launching surprise attacks, their vessels being lighter and more manoeuvrable in shallow waters. England eventually emerged victorious, however, because their ships were stouter, and mounted heavier guns; and in the later engagements better seamanship showed through. The wars fell into three periods: 1651–54, 1665–67 and 1672–74, and were concerned with control of the seas for the purposes of keeping open the trade routes, mainly in the East Indies; other countries learned stark lessons from these battles.

The Battle of the Dunes, 1658

Coming in the middle of these wars, the English navy would show how it was possible for naval artillery to provide covering fire in support of land operations. In 1658 the French king, Louis XIV, was fighting a war against the Habsburgs over the claim to the Spanish throne. French forces were besieging the town of Dunkirk throughout May and June that year, and were expecting a reinforcement column of at least 15,000 men, under Marshal Vicomte de Turenne. Instead an English naval force arrived off the coast, from which 3,000 men, commanded by Sir William Lockhart, disembarked to join the fighting against the Spanish forces in the Netherlands. What has come to be called the Battle of the Dunes was fought on 14 June 1658, and the action showed new tactical uses for naval artillery. On the morning of the battle, Turenne deployed his troops in two lines across the dunes, with the English on his left flank. The Spanish army of some 14,000, under joint command of Don Juan of Austria and the Great Condé of Spain, was drawn up in formation with its right flank resting on the beach.

The English forces attacked the Spanish right flank, during which action they were supported by artillery fire from their ships. The Spanish had not wanted to commit their forces for fear of this happening, and by the time they deployed their cavalry it was too late. French cavalry, led by the Marquis Jacques de Castelnau, attacked and forced them to withdraw. The battle lasted four hours and produced a complete victory for Turenne, and by nightfall Dunkirk was captured. It was given to Oliver Cromwell in recognition for his support in the war. Naval artillery had shown how it could be used with an imaginative commander to support an army during coastal operations. The Battle of the Dunes laid down the rules of engagement for such actions, and these would be repeated many times in different wars around the world.

THE WEIGHT OF FIREPOWER

The English navy had always relied on weight of firepower to defeat the enemy. During the war against Spain – which saw the defeat of the Spanish Armada of 1588 – it was the sheer weight of artillery fire, coupled with adverse weather, which provided England with a great victory. The Spanish had an over-dependency on soldiers to the detriment of artillery, and the fact that Spain did not fully realize the importance of the ship as a gun platform is evident when one considers that the fighting force of the Armada comprised 19,000 soldiers and only 8,000 sailors. The English navy, on the other hand, had used its guns to break up the Spanish formation. Typically, English gunners could fire three times for every shot fired by the Spanish, with every round finding a target.

The type of gun being mounted on ships had moved away from the old type secured to a flat wooden platform, and with the introduction of trunnions, barrels could now be securely fitted to wooden carriages mounted on four small wheels, and known as trucks. The trunnions, set back at about four-sevenths of the barrel length from the muzzle, slotted into recesses and were kept in place by bands of iron, called cap squares, that were pinned to the carriage. This secured the barrel to the carriage and allowed the weapon to be moved quickly and easily.

The barrel, with its thickened and heavier breech end, meant that the muzzle was always

A cannon mounted on a wooden carriage, such as was used to arm warships in the seventeenth century. They could also be used in coastal fortifications.

elevated, and wooden wedges had to be placed under the breech end to lower the muzzle. In order to complete this action the gunners had to use wooden levers to lift the breech end. The wooden carriages or trucks had side pieces or 'cheeks' constructed in a stepped design that allowed the crews to use these as fulcrums when using their lever, which made the operation much easier.

The barrels of drakes could be much shorter than other designs of artillery. For example, the barrel length of a 'culverin bastard' as used on the *Mary Rose*, the pride of the fleet for King Henry VIII, was almost 10ft (3m), but for a saker drake in the seventeenth century the barrel was only about 4ft (1m) in length, and even the larger culverin drake had a barrel just 8.5ft (2.5m) in length. This meant that such weapons were much easier to handle in the small confines of the gun deck on warships of the day. They were also quicker to reload because they were much shorter, but they did not compromise weight of shot. The saker drake, for example, could fire a 5lb (2.2kg) solid shot, and this was comparable to an ordinary saker that weighed 1,900lb (862kg) and more than twice its length. These weapons fired spherical cast-iron shot, which had by now replaced stone projectiles. There were also other specialist projectiles being introduced, specifically for use at sea.

Testing Round Shot

To appreciate the effectiveness of round shot against the wooden hulls of ships, one only has to refer to the trials completed by John Greaves, Professor of Geometry at Gresham College in March 1651. The trials were conducted at Woolwich, and involved the use of guns of various calibre firing against three target butts constructed of 19in (48cm) of oak and elm, with a gap of 42ft (12.8m) between the first and second butt, and 24ft (7.3m) between the second and third butt. A 32lb (14.5kg) projectile fired from an iron demi-cannon penetrated the first two butts and hit the third. An 18lb (8kg) projectile fired from a brass culverin with a barrel length of 11ft (3.3m), with a charge of 10lb (4.5kg) of powder also penetrated the first two butts, but failed to hit the third. The range of trials continued and showed how the wooden hulls of warships could be smashed.

Results of similar trials conducted by Sieur de Gaya in Spain during 1678, showed how a round-shot projectile could penetrate 24ft (7.3m) of light sand, 17ft (5m) of packed earth, and 12ft (3.6m) of embankment at a range of 200yd (183m). All these trials proved that if ships could bring their guns to bear on a target they could devastate it, and even be used to engage and reduce coastal defence batteries.

STANDARD PROJECTILES

The standard projectile was the solid iron ball, which, on impacting the wooden sides of the ships, produced large splinters that flew off and inflicted terrible injuries on the gun crews. Specialized projectiles were developed later in order to attack the rigging and masts of ships. These included expanding bar shot, chain shot and star, all of which were intended to shred the sails and rigging of the enemy ship. Once these parts of the ship had been torn away by gunfire it could not manoeuvre, and the attacker could pound away until it had destroyed its target. Chain shot consisted of two halves of a cannon ball connected by a length of chain, and loaded as a complete projectile; on firing, the halves would separate and swirl in a flailing action, which tore through ropes and sail. It could also dismember a man or cut him in half.

There was a variation on this design, with the ball being sectioned into quarters, which also produced fearful injuries. The expanding bar shot was like a telescopic plunger: it was loaded as a single projectile, and on exiting the muzzle, it expanded along its own length. The trajectory it followed was a tumbling or flailing action, and on hitting the target it inflicted the same type of damage as produced by chain shot. The 'star' shot was similar in principle, but had four radial arms instead of just one long bar. Sir Jonas Moore's writings of the period confirm the use of such projectiles at close quarters.

Added to these projectiles was langridge, a collection of musket balls, nails, and other sundry small objects such as stones. This was used from a variety of weapons, such as fowlers, slings or bases, and designed to be used at close quarters for anti-personnel actions in clearing the enemy. These weapons were referred to collectively as 'murdering pieces' and the langridge fired from them was: '...like unto a lanthern full of pobble stones, dice shot, musket bullets, pieces of iron or suchlike will doe great execution.' These light pieces of close-quarter artillery were fitted to swivelling mounts and would be used on ships wherever trade routes were being contested.

In the Far East such weapons were called lantaka and made of brass, and the mass of projectiles were like an early form of grapeshot or canister shot.

On its truck carriage the angle of the barrel could be altered by means of inserting or removing wooden wedges, which in turn adjusted the firing range. It was all very rudimentary, and aiming was still performed very much by line of sight. The ship would be pitching up and down, rolling from side to side, and all the while sailing forward on its course. Loading was very hazardous, and the prospect of having so much volatile material in the form of gunpowder and naked flames was not something anyone cared to dwell on for too long.

The Risks On Board

Many times accidents were recorded involving the spontaneous ignition of gunpowder leading to the destruction of ships. In 1512, whilst fighting a close-quarter action against the *Marie la Cordière* off the coast of Brest, the English ship the *Regent* was sunk when the gunpowder stores of the French vessel exploded. Ships were self-contained arsenals, storing projectiles and gunpowder on board, and some vessels had hundreds of barrels of gunpowder in magazines. If these caught fire the consequences were catastrophic, which in the case above resulted in 600 English deaths and over 1,000 French deaths. Francis Markham, an author on artillery who wrote a book in 1622 entitled *The Five Decades of Epistles of Warre*, related how he heard of a fatal accident on board an unnamed vessel, which involved a 'canonière' who was the worse for drink. Allegedly the man had dropped his linstock, the lighted match for igniting the priming powder on a cannon, into a barrel containing gunpowder. The accident killed the man outright, seriously injured others, and badly damaged the ship.

CONTROLLING THE GUN

Several navies at the time quickly realized that if the wooden carriages were tethered to the walls of the ship's gun deck, then it would be possible to control the recoil force and use it to the benefit of the gun crew. Recoil was the force produced on firing that made the gun roll back on its own length. Due to the fact that ships tended to engage in battle at fairly close ranges, the charges of gunpowder were often less powerful than those that would be loaded into guns firing on land.

Nevertheless, the guns still had to be restrained, to prevent them rolling across the decks out of control. Through an ingenious series of pulleys and ropes the gun carriage could be checked in its recoil after being fired. Referred to as breeching ropes, they allowed the crew to haul the gun into place and 'run it out' so that the muzzle emerged through the gun port. On firing, the gun could only recoil as far as the ropes would permit it. Most naval guns by this period were muzzle-loaded, and on being reloaded the crew hauled on the ropes to place it back into its firing position. If the weapon had to be traversed, this was done so by means of 'gun spikes', stout wooden poles to literally lever the gun into position. As firing techniques improved, so the barrels of naval cannon developed to suit the role. At the thickened breech end an 'eye' or ring was developed, called a cascable; one of the breeching ropes passed through this fitting and permitted easier handling. For the first time the gun crews had some degree of control over the guns during all stages of firing.

Iron cannon mounted on a wooden carriage, of the type used by warships. The design could also be used in coastal defence to engage maritime targets.

Artillery on land did not have this feature because the guns were mounted on larger-wheeled carriages and there was more room for recoil on the battlefield.

GUN CREWS: TRAINING AND MAINTENANCE

Crews of warships in the seventeenth century were by this time competently trained, and standing officers lived on board. One of these new officer classes included the master gunner who was responsible for the readiness of guns in time of war and the preparedness of the gun crews. The sailors were mariners first, and trained as gunners for the time of war; they were paid at a rate equal to 50 pence per month, and an inventory of 1602 informs us that the cost of keeping a 900-ton English warship at sea with forty gunners for one month was over £750. For a 48-ton ship with only five gunners, the same document tells us that it cost over £45 to keep the ship at sea for the same period. In 1665, the naval force of England stood at 160 warships mounting 500 guns with 25,000 sailors, and inevitably this placed an enormous strain on the economy. At the time the Dutch naval force numbered 133 vessels, so the size of the English navy was justified if the country was to be protected.

In his work *The Arte of Shooting in Great Ordnaunce* William Bourne points out the importance of controlling the ship whilst the guns were in action. One section states '...he that is at the Helme must be sure to steere steady and bee ruled by him that giveth the levell, and he that giveth fire must be nimble and ready at a suddaine.' The general belief of the day was that it required one man per 500lb (227kg) of gun on board ship; this meant that a gun weighing 6,600lb (3,000kg) firing a projectile weighing 32lb (14.5kg) required a gun crew of thirteen men. However, it should be remembered that not every gun had its own crew, and only those guns firing towards the enemy would be served, which meant that only half the guns on board were in action at any one time. Very rarely would a ship find itself in a position where guns on both sides had to fire at the same time. If this were the case, then the gun crews would alternate between guns on the starboard (right) and those on the port side (left).

GUN DRILL AND FIRING TECHNIQUE

Each member of the gun crew had a specific function in the operation of the gun, in exactly the same way as the gunners on the battlefield. However, on board ship the urgency of good gun drills could mean the difference between victory and defeat, or worse still, being sunk. Taking the 6,600lb gun as an example, with its crew of thirteen, they served the gun in the following manner: Number One was the captain of the gun and controlled its operation. Number Two was designated as second captain who would oversee operations should anything happen to the Number One. Numbers Three and Four were loader and sponger respectively. Numbers Five, Six, Seven and Eight were detailed to operate the side tackles to run out the gun for firing, and generally keep it in firing position. Numbers Nine and Ten were equipped with handspikes to move the gun from side to side for adjustment. Number Eleven primed the gun by pouring fine powder into the vent ready for firing. Number Twelve brought the shot and wadding to the gun. Number Thirteen was designated as 'powderman', and as such had to supply the cartridge box. The confined space on the gun decks meant that all actions were performed in a crouched-over manner, which hampered speed.

Muzzle-loaded guns required everything to be inserted into the barrel via the muzzle opening. Originally, a long-handled ladle with a scoop or bowl of either wood or copper was used to load powder into the barrel, which was then rammed down into the chamber. However, it was realized very early that the restricted working space between decks slowed down this operation, and in battle that was unacceptable. Therefore, prepared charges in bags were introduced, which meant that it was a straightforward case of inserting a single charge and then ramming that well into the chamber. These were termed 'cartridges', and made handling powder safer. Old rope was used as wadding between powder charge and projectile. The crewman serving the vent had to pierce the cartridge bag with a small spike before pouring some fine powder into the vent to 'prime' the gun ready for firing. Using a slow match or taper, fire was then applied to the vent, and the gun discharged. The sponge man would then move forward and swab out the barrel with a wet sponge to extinguish any smouldering debris left in the barrel that might ignite the next charge as it was loaded.

When the new cartridge was inserted into the barrel, one man had to place his finger over the vent hole in an action called 'serving the vent'. This was to prevent air being sucked into the barrel during the ramming action, which might in turn ignite smouldering debris and cause a premature explosion. Contrary to popular belief the crewman performing this action did not use his thumb, but rather his middle finger. The reason for this was that, should there be an accidental flaring from the vent and the man lost his thumb he would not be able to pick up any object; but if it were his middle finger he would still be able to manipulate objects. The same function was performed with land-based artillery.

TYPES OF ARTILLERY DEPLOYED AT SEA

The Chase Cannon

The use of cartridge by naval gunners is explained by Sir Jonas Moore around 1689, who tells us: 'Upon the sea, to load great ordnance they never load with a ladle, but make use of cartridges, as well for security, in not firing the powder, which in time of fight is in continual motion.' Sir Jonas also tells of the effectiveness of the 'chase cannon' used to fire on an enemy ship being pursued, referring to these weapons as corsiere, cannon, and the chase cannon, of which there could be up to nine guns mounted in the bows of a galley. He claims it was the weapon mounted in the centre and firing directly over the stem that was the most accurate, '...which in time of fight doth the most effectual service'. He goes on to say how the recoil of the weapon was along the length of deck, '...along the middle of the gally to the mast, where they place some soft substance to hinder its farther recoil, that it might not endammage the mast'. His writings thus tell us that the chase gun lacked proper tackle ropes to check its recoil, and he also confirms the structure of the four-wheel truck carriages, which could be run out through the gun ports.

The Bomb Ketch

Apart from the standard guns mounted in the sides of warships, which fired at the target along line of sight – meaning that the target had to be visible if it was to be attacked – there were other types of artillery deployed at sea, designed to fulfil a specialized role. One such type to make the transfer was the mortar that the French mounted in specially constructed vessels known as 'bomb ketches' or 'bomb vessels'. This combination was used by the French from 1680, and by 1693 England was following suit, when they were referred to as 'H.M. bombs'. These were vessels with a very shallow draft so they could sail as close to the coast as possible in order to bombard the coastal defences from very short range. Being armed with mortars, the projectiles they fired had a very high angle of trajectory in order to reach over the walls and earthworks of an installation. Written works covering this form of naval artillery were published as instructions, one of which was the French reference called *The Art of Throwing Bombs* that appeared in 1699 and covered siege warfare, and the role of the navy in such warfare.

The Mortar

Mortars had been in use as augmentation weapons in the range of artillery for some time, but their employment at sea was new. Sir Jonas Moore noted how mortars in the seventeenth century could '...shoot balls of

Iron barrel cannon mounted on a wooden carriage of the type used in seventeenth-century warships. Note the wooden wheels and the wooden wedge used to adjust the angle of the barrel.

stone, Grando-shels, and cases full of small shot, not by a Right line but by a crooked from on high so they fall where it should be appointed'. With this observation he is explaining that mortars did not fire by line of sight directly at the target, but instead by indirect fire which 'lobbed' the shell in a high arc. This meant that projectiles, especially the hollow shell filled with gunpowder, could be fired over the walls of coastal defences. The vessels designed to carry these relatively short-range mortars had to be built to an incredibly strong design, because the hull had to absorb all the recoil forces directly. The mortars mounted in such vessels tended to be much larger than their counterparts used on land, and calibres up to 13in (33cm) were not uncommon. The projectiles used were of the explosive type, designed to detonate inside the target area.

Gauging the optimum length of fuse was the main difficulty, and exactly when and how to ignite it was also a problem. The fuses for these 'bombs' were made from tubes of either willow or birch filled with fine gunpowder. Some gunners advocated lighting the fuse before firing the main charge, while others loaded the bomb so that the fuse was next to the main propellant charge; that way, when the weapon was fired the fuse would ignite. At least that was the theory. However, it did not always work properly, and the fuse could be dislodged on firing. If the mortar bomb landed before the fuse had burnt through, the defenders might extinguish it, if they were quick enough and brave enough to approach the device. And if the fuse detonated the bomb before it reached its target, it was a wasted shot. Discovering a solution to this perennial problem of fusing did not come quickly or easily, but when it was finally resolved the use of mortars on both land and sea revolutionized artillery tactics.

A Transitional Stage

Naval artillery during the seventeenth century went through a transitional stage, and a number of countries began to experiment with various designs and practices in gunnery. In 1665 the English warship *Swiftsure* was armed with seventy-two guns, of which sixty were brass and only twelve of iron. By 1700, despite the expense, English warships were increasingly armed with brass guns. It was not only the weaponry itself that changed, but also the form of warfare. When a Dutch fleet under Michiel de Ruyter attacked the defences covering the River Medway in 1667 during the Second Anglo-Dutch War, he came within twenty miles (thirty-two kilometres) of London, having succeeded in sinking several major warships along the way. The attack highlighted the need to improve on coastal defences and build better emplacements, and to train gun crews to engage naval targets. This was something that all nations with a coastal region could learn by, and build their own defences accordingly.

BATTLE TECHNIQUE FOR FIGHTING SHIPS

The sailing-ship design of the seventeenth century would remain unaltered for almost two hundred years until the introduction of steam-powered ships. But despite their awesome firepower, the reputation of these floating gun platforms was greater than the results they could deliver in battle. Not all naval engagements ended with ships being sunk due to gunfire. For example, Professor Lewis in his work *The History of the British Navy* points out that between 1692 and 1782 there were fifteen 'line' battles employing standard tactics, but they failed to produce the sinking of a single enemy ship. One of the reasons for this was that fighting ships took up formation in line ahead so that each vessel took on its opposite number in the enemy line formation. This practice had been detailed in the work *Fighting Instructions*, published in 1653 and later amended in 1673. These tactics would remain as the set tactical procedure for almost 150 years, and ships' captains would not depart from these instructions if they valued their command. It wasn't until the end of the eighteenth century and into the early nineteenth century that commanders such as Admiral Lord Nelson broke with convention and showed how versatile gunnery could be, and brought about decisive victories.

10 Tools and the Artillery Train

The families of gunners still accompanied them on campaign, and also served as assistants. Here, a recreated scene shows how gunners made their lives around their weapons and guarded them at all times.

At this time a certain rivalry between the infantry and the artillery was beginning to emerge, in which the infantry accused the artillerymen of conceit and of adopting superior graces. For their part the gunners took great pride in their appearance, maintaining high levels of cleanliness and maintenance of their weapons. During the English Civil War, for example, the gunners of the New Model Army painted the carriages of their artillery grey: this was referred to as being 'Fair Ledd colour', and thereby set a trend for uniformity. This livery also helped in the identification of the force on the battlefield, and the smartness of this appearance reflected the professionalism of the gunners.

Regardless of any opinions held by the infantry, the gunners had to operate their weapons to a strict set of rules. For example, there were thirteen commands governing the loading and firing of artillery. A typical field gun at the time of the English Civil War was operated by a crew of at least three men: the gunner, the gunner's mate, still called a mattross, and an assistant who was used for the fetching and carrying.

Some men held deep-rooted superstitions; for instance, it was considered a 'foul fault for a gunner to commit' if an artilleryman scooped out the incorrect charge of gunpowder from the budge barrel. And if gunpowder was spilled on the ground he should not stand on it, for such an action was regarded as 'it being a thing uncomely for a gunner to trample powder under his feet'. This observation was really a safety point, because the friction could spontaneously ignite the gunpowder, with disastrous consequences. Gunners were also expected to conduct themselves in a manner which 'set forth himself with as comely a posture and grace as he can: for agility and comely

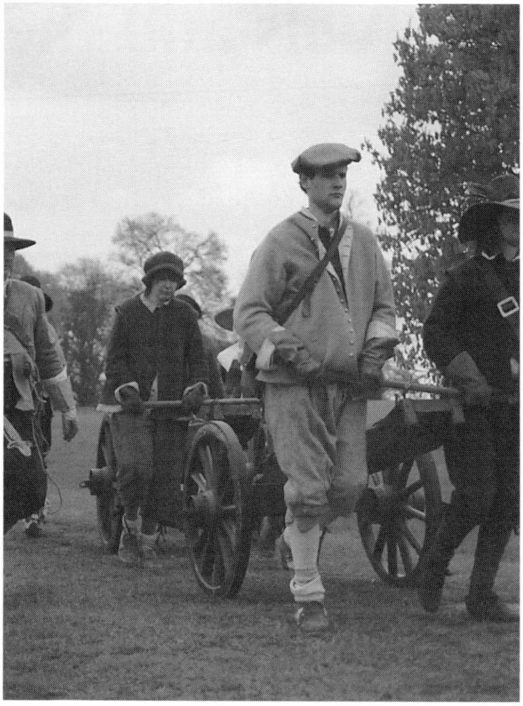

Recreated method of how gunners in the seventeenth century moved their artillery and the wagons containing gunpowder.

Dover Castle in Kent where master gunner William Eldred conducted many trials with various types of artillery, including 'Queen Elizabeth's Pocket Pistol'. The castle was held by a Royalist garrison during the English Civil War.

carriage in handling the ladle and sponge doth he give great content to standers by'. This was to show that he was a professional and competent gunner and as such could be relied on for his steadfastness in battle.

One of the most influential books to be written on the subject of artillery during the seventeenth century was entitled *The Gunner's Glasse*. The author was William Eldred, who at one time had been master gunner to Dover Castle in Kent. The publication date is given as being either 1642 or 1646, by which time Eldred was at least eighty-three years of age. His work lists many observations, and also his trials with various pieces of artillery, each of which had been arrived at with a degree of valid reasoning behind them. For example, Eldred states that the average rate of fire should be no more than eight shots in one hour. He continues by writing that after firing forty shots the gun should be allowed to cool for one hour. He furthermore believed that eighty shots continuous would create too much heat and cause the gun to fail by exploding on firing. These guidelines are, of course, safety margins, but they had more than a modicum of sense to them. If the metal of a weapon holds too much heat after prolonged firing then it is likely to cause a spontaneous or premature detonation as the propellant charge is loaded, even if the barrel has been well swabbed before loading.

GUN DRILLS FOR A LAND BATTLE

Just as with the gun drills for loading artillery at sea, so Eldred lists the commands and drills for loading a 'peece' of artillery during a land battle. His work must, therefore, be seen as a training manual as much as anything else.

1. 'Put back your peece': assuming the gun has been fired, this means to return the gun to its original position. It can also be taken to mean that the gun should be put into its firing position in readiness for action.
2. 'Order your peece to load': the gunners would remove the elevating wedge from under the breech end, which being the heaviest part of gun, would automatically raise the muzzle, thereby making it easier to load.
3. 'Search you peece': a member of the gun crew would select either a worm or a half-moon and insert it into the barrel in order to remove any fouling or smouldering embers from previous firings.
4. 'Sponge your peece': one of the crew would use a long-handled tool with a wad of wet rags to mop out the interior of the barrel to extinguish any smouldering debris which may have been overlooked. This action would only be completed between shots; it also assisted in cooling the barrel slightly, and prevented any premature detonation of the gunpowder charge when loaded.
5. 'Fill you ladle': these long-handled wooden tools, looking a bit like oversized spoons, often had increments inscribed on them to indicate the load of gunpowder to be used on a particular gun. The crewman would fill the ladle to the required level.
6. 'Put in your powder': the powder loader would insert the ladle into the barrel through the muzzle.
7. 'Empty your ladle': the man would then rotate the handle to invert the bowl and tip the powder charge into the breech.
8. 'Put home your powder': this order instructed a man to use a wooden rammer

Recreated seventeenth-century field gun mounted on a wooden carriage. Note the gunners standing in readiness with rammers and swabs to reload the weapon.

in a thrusting motion to tamper down the loose powder in the breech to eliminate air pockets. At this stage a man would 'serve the vent', which in some drill books specified placing a thumb over the vent hole through which the propellant charge would be ignited.

9. 'Thrust home your wad': this instructed the loader to insert a bundle of combustible fibrous material such as grass, straw or old rags. The intention of this was to hold back the expanding gases of the powder charge on ignition just a fraction of a second. This delay allowed the propelling gases to build up pressure to begin the process of expelling the ball from the barrel. The flash and heat on being fired would burn away the wadding material. It was the residue of this that had to be wet sponged in order to extinguish it before re-loading.
10. 'Regard your shot': the gunner had to examine the cannon ball before inserting it into the barrel. This was to make sure it was of the correct calibre, and to allow sufficient clearance to load the projectile without the unnecessary use of force. This clearance was called 'windage', and the optimum gap was never more than 0.25in (1/4in, or 0.64cm). If there were too much gap, then much of the propellant force would be expended uselessly as it vented forwards past the projectile. The correct fitting, therefore, of the projectile was vitally important for both accuracy and velocity.
11. 'Put home your shot gently': the projectile was rammed home securely, but not too hard, so as to avoid over-compression of the powder charge in the chamber. If the powder were compacted tightly it would not burn at a regular rate, and produced a poor shot or a misfire.
12. 'Thrust home your last wad with three thrusts': this was another fibrous wad of combustible material. It was inserted into the barrel after the projectile, and was intended to prevent the cannon ball from

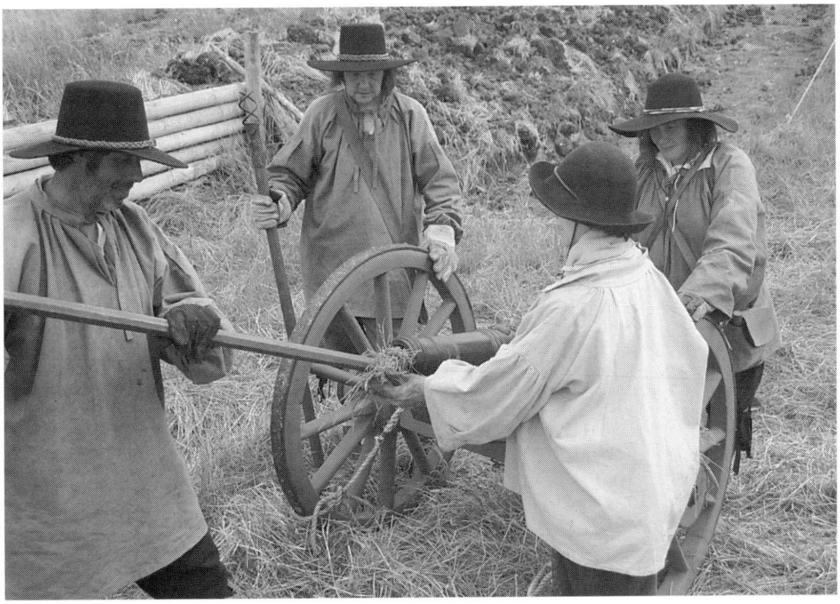

A gun crew prepares and loads a recreated seventeenth-century field gun in the type of firing positions that would have been used on the battlefield, if time permitted such preparations.

The moment of firing a recreated seventeenth-century field gun, showing great clouds of smoke enveloping the scene as they must have done in battle for real.

rolling out of the barrel if the carriage had to be moved to realign to a target.

13. 'Gauge your piece': on this order the cannon was aimed at the target. The gunners would elevate the barrel and move the carriage left or right to align it with the target. The gunner's quadrant would be used to calculate the range, and only now was it ready to fire.

Once all these tasks had been completed, the gunner then 'primed the vent', when a small

Recreated artillery showing gunners in their various positions for operating the guns on the battlefield.

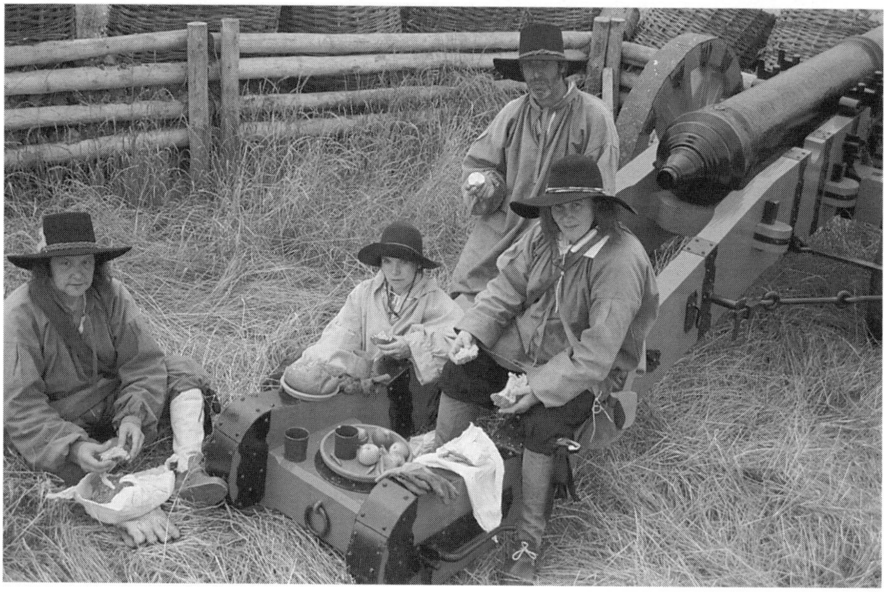

Gunners not only fired their guns in battle, they also lived in close proximity to the weapon, as seen here in this recreated scene. This association meant that each gun had its own permanent guard to protect it.

quantity of very fine gunpowder, known as 'mealed' powder, was trickled into the chamber. The firer then applied a slow match to the vent, which ignited and burned through to set off the main charge in the chamber. This method of loading and firing would last as long as muzzle-loading artillery was in use, well into the late nineteenth century. If one considers Eldred's loading procedure to be protracted, it should be remembered that the loading and firing drills covering the use of 'matchlock' muskets ran to more than thirty separate instructions. However, all these instructions were 'according to the drill manual', and a well

Recreated drake minion being loaded by the crew as it would have been on the battlefield in the seventeenth century.

trained and motivated gun crew could load and fire without hesitation. In battle these actions came as second nature to an experienced crew, and they could perform their duties without orders.

Gun crews sometimes adapt the drill book instructions to produce what they thought were better results. One such change was that covering the instruction for the man detailed to 'serve the vent', according to number eight in Eldred's list of instructions. To serve the vent, in theory, a man was required to place his thumb over the vent to stop any draught of air through the vent hole thereby preventing any smouldering powder or fragment from the wadding being ignited. The tell-tale sign for a gunner involved in this operation was usually a split thumb. To prevent this painful condition the vent man was issued with a 'thumb-stall', a small leather tube that was slipped over the thumb and tied around the wrist. In practice, however, a man would place a finger over the vent. The reason for this is simply that if there were an accident involving ignition of the powder and the man lost his thumb he would not be able to pick up any object. However, if he lost a finger through an accident during this process, he could still articulate objects in his hand. This technique was also practised by gunners at sea, and continued to be routine drill until the nineteenth century when muzzle-loading cannons were phased out of service.

THE 'TOOLS OF THE TRADE'

By now, gunners were beginning to use items of equipment that were becoming recognised as being standard across the branch of artillery. These were seen as being special 'tools of the trade' for gunners, with no real application outside the artillery force. For example the stiletto, a dagger with a finely pointed blade, believed to have originated in Italy, was intended for use by gunners to measure the calibre of guns and projectiles by using a scale engraved on the blade. The

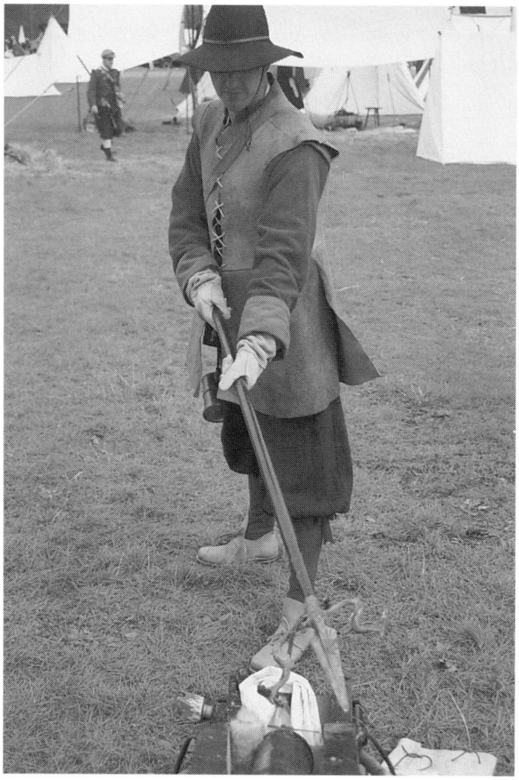

Recreated gunner prepares to fire the weapon by applying the match to the vent. He is using a device called a linstock, which held the burning match to ignite the fine powder at the vent. This was a tool in universal use by gunners throughout the period.

A range of instruments used by gunners of the seventeenth century. On the gun carriage is the gunners' quadrant used for sighting the barrel and the swab for cleaning the barrel between firings, and the man is using a linstock to fire the gun.

blades of stilettos for artillery were triangular in section and engraved with a scale that allowed gunners to convert the measurements of calibre to weight of shot and so calculate the charge of powder required to fire the weapon. A variation of this device, known as the 'gunner's rule' was developed in seventeenth-century England. This instrument, as with the dagger-like stiletto, could be used to convert the calibre of a projectile to obtain its weight and work out the charge of gunpowder required for a particular gun.

The Portfire

In order to fire the guns safely, a system known as the 'portfire' was developed. The name is believed to have been taken from the French term '*porte-feu*', and Anglicized to 'portfire'. Made in varying lengths, but usually around 16in (40cm), it was also referred to as the quick-match. The portfire was made from a cord that had been dipped in a solution of spirits and saltpetre and coated with finely mealed or corned powder. When the battery was ordered to commence firing, the gunner

Recreated seventeenth-century gunner showing the detail of the linstock that was used to hold the lighted match for application to the vent in order to fire the gun.

Recreated seventeenth-century gunners standing by a saker-drake, with other paraphernalia associated with artillery. This includes a water bucket for swabbing out the barrel between firings, and other tools such as the linstock and runners.

would light his portfire from the slow-match: this was also made from a cord dipped in a mixture of spirits and saltpetre, but given a coating of melted sulphur. This slow-match was left burning continuously, and was held in the spring-loaded jaws of a clamp set on a wooden pole and known as the linstock. One slow-match on a linstock would be placed between two guns. Such a practice kept the sources of naked flames to a minimum until battle commenced, and was a safety point considering the amount of gunpowder kept within the battery positions.

On being given the command to fire, a gunner would apply his portfire to the fine powder in the vent of the gun. This would burn through and ignite the main propelling charge, which

The gunner wearing a helmet is shown holding a linstock used to hold the fuse that was applied to the touch-hole to fire the weapon.

would in turn detonate and fire the cannon ball from the barrel. When ordered to stop firing, the gunners would cut the burning tip off the portfire with special cutters, thereby preserving the unburned remains of the portfire.

The portfire was a great improvement to safety, but it did not entirely replace the linstock as the means of firing the guns. In an emergency the linstock holding the slow-match could be applied to the vent for firing the gun.

Specialized Tools

Some of the implements used by gunners, such as the rammer and the sponge for swabbing out the barrel after firing, had obvious applications. But some tools were less identifiable, such as the worm, which was fitted with two spirals of metal like a twin-pronged fork, and used for clearing obstructions from the barrel. The half-moon was another specialized tool, used to 'scour' the barrel with a semi-circular disc fitted to a long wooden handle. This device removed any build-up of carbon-fouling left inside the barrel after firing, which might otherwise prevent proper loading. All these tools, such as the powder scoop, were fitted with long wooden handles and, apart from varying in length, were very much in universal usage with gunners around the world.

The Quadrant

Through printed works such as books and pamphlets, an increasing number of gunners were beginning to understand the important relationship between the weight of the charge of gunpowder loaded into the chamber, and the angle of elevation to which the barrel was set. They realized that these two conditions determined how far the cannon ball travelled when

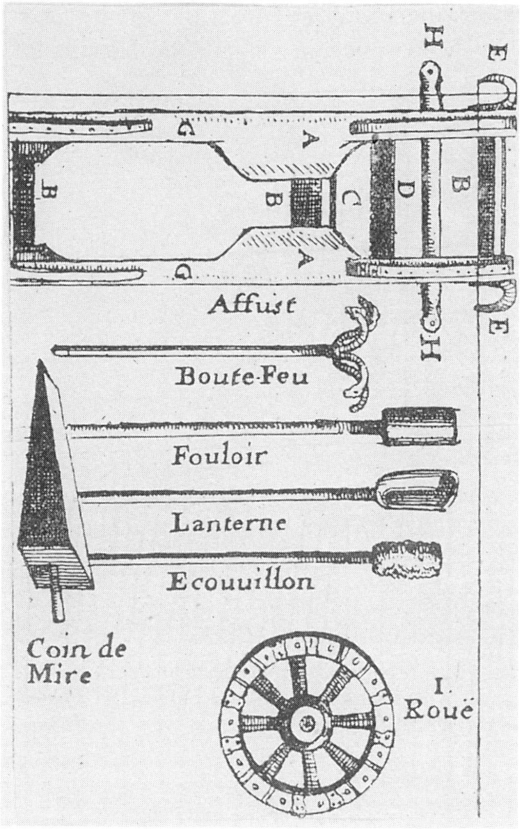

A range of gunners' tools used for loading, including sponges, rammers and ladles used for inserting charges of gunpowder. Also shown is a detail of a gun carriage and wheel design. The wooden wedge was used for elevating the barrel.

fired; but they also realized that the powder charge in such instances had to be a properly calculated weight, and that the angle of elevation was given by measurements arrived at through use of the gunner's quadrant. Gunnery was now becoming a precise science, and success on the battlefield depended on the accuracy of the artillery: thus in order to maintain their high standard of professionalism and special status, gunners had to use proper drills and correct calculations. The quadrant gave them the potential to engage targets with precise

Recreated gunner of the seventeenth century showing how the quadrant would have been used to sight the barrel before firing. The instrument was invaluable to the artillerymen of the day.

measurements. The device came in many forms, but always with divisions or points marked off in mathematical angles, and in use it was always set to a right-angle pattern, which gave ninety degrees.

Developed by Niccolo Targtaglia in the sixteenth century, the gunner's quadrant had, by the seventeenth century, come to be an invaluable tool for the artillery. By inserting one end of the quadrant into the muzzle of the barrel so that the quadrant faced down, the attached weighted cord cut across the angles of elevation, from which a reading could then be taken. The gunner then elevated or depressed — that is to say, raised or lowered — the barrel, until the cord indicated the scale at the correct point for the required range.

Moving the barrel of the gun was still very rudimentary, and did not give a precise angle of elevation. Although the elevating screw had been developed in the sixteenth century, some armies still altered the angle of the barrel by using handspikes and wooden wedges, called quoins. These wedges were either inserted or removed between the rear portion of the carriage and the breech end of the barrel to adjust the elevation of the muzzle. Aiming a line at a specific point was still a question of aligning the gun in the general direction and firing at the intended target. This was known as 'gun laying', and it required a certain amount of brute force to manoeuvre the gun carriage on its wheels by means of handspikes in order to lever the gun into position. In this respect, it was not dissimilar from artillery practices at sea.

GUNPOWDER AND BAGGED CHARGES

The constituents of gunpowder had also changed over the period since it was first described by Friar Roger Bacon in around 1250. In those early days the composition of gunpowder was very coarse, comprising 41.2 per cent saltpetre and 29.4 per cent each of charcoal and sulphur. By the seventeenth century many countries had master gunners who developed their own preferred formula. One of the variations to be produced appeared in 1647, during the English Civil War, when master gunner Nye experimented in trying to produce a better mixture of gunpowder. The formula he developed consisted

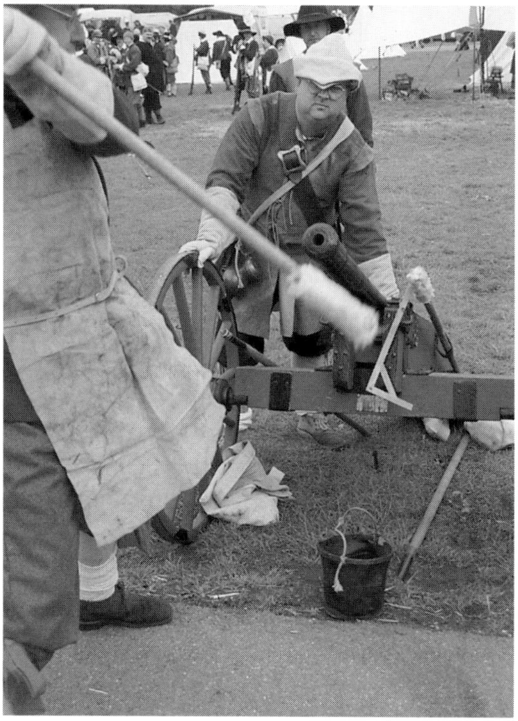

Gunners preparing to sponge or 'swab' out the barrel between firings in order to prevent accidental explosions. These are recreated in the most authentic manner, and are an accurate portrayal of the period.

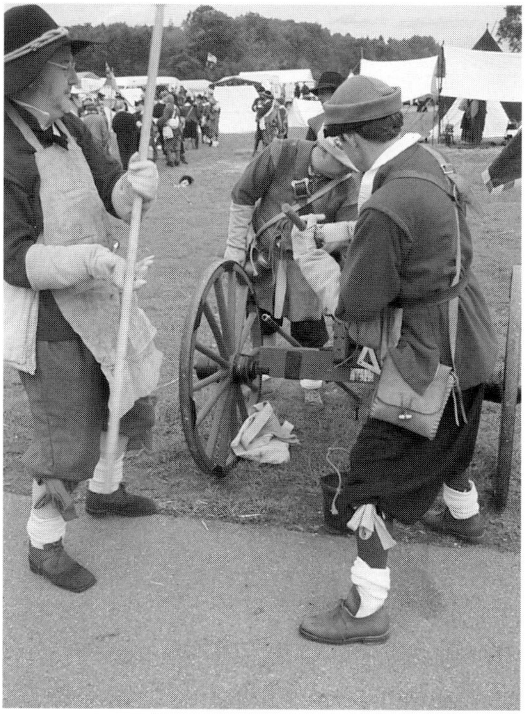

Recreated gunners of the seventeenth century preparing their gun for loading. They are using authentic-style tools as the gunners of the period would have used. Note the man on the left is wearing a leather apron in order to prevent any gunpowder from contaminating his clothing, thus preventing an accident.

of 66.6 per cent saltpetre, and 16.6 per cent each for charcoal and sulphur. In 1670 Sir J. Turner developed the mixture of 71.4 per cent saltpetre and 14.3 per cent each for charcoal and sulphur. It is interesting to note that in 1653 saltpetre, the main constituent of gunpowder, was 9d per pound, but thirty-one years later, in 1684, the price had fallen to 6d per pound. Supply and demand would make the price of gunpowder fluctuate throughout the seventeenth century.

The method of using 'bagged' charges of gunpowder is generally credited as being developed by Gustavus Adolphus of Sweden. Whether or not he personally developed the use of bagged charges, or was merely responsible for overseeing their introduction into service, is not exactly clear, but the advantages of using pre-prepared charges of powder had long been realized. Given time beforehand, a gunner was well advised to prepare charges of powder for loading, as this would greatly speed up his rate of firing. In the closing years of the sixteenth century gunners had been advised thus:

> ...if a gunner charge his piece with cartredges he ought to sett them upright in a

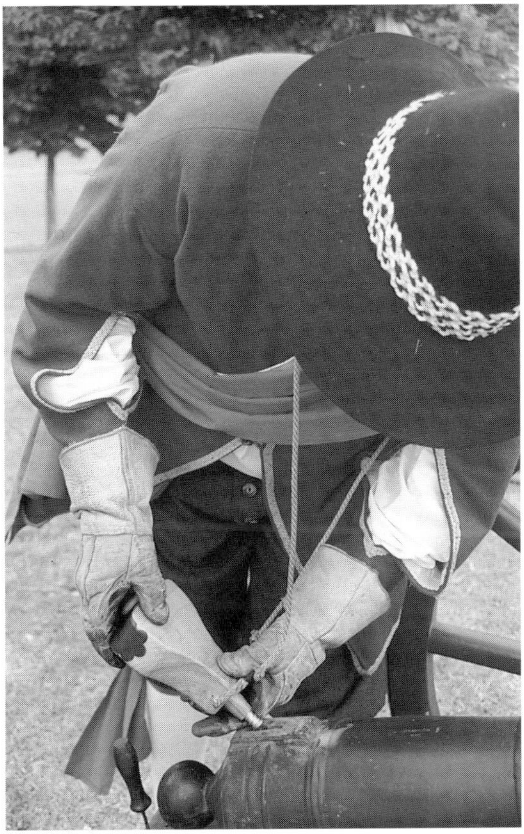

> tubb or some other wooden vessel, which (though it seem to stand in a place out of danger for fire) should never be uncovered for any longer time than while the same cartredges are taken out one by one to charge the piece…

This method of loading gunpowder into paper or linen pouches known as cartridges had first been used by musketeers, and it was only natural that this technique was adopted by the artillery to minimize the risk of accidental explosion in handling loose powder during battle.

Artillery using bagged charges prepared in advance increased the speed with which the opening salvo could be fired, and would, it was hoped, catch the enemy at a disadvantage.

Gunner making a cannon ready to fire. He is shown here priming the touch-hole of an artillery piece by applying a charge of finely corned gunpowder to the vent in preparation to firing the weapon.

Falconet being prepared to fire by gunners using recreated authentic tools of the trade.

If the battle progressed beyond the point where the gunners had fired off all their prepared charges, they had to resort to ladling loose gunpowder from the budge barrels into the gun chamber. This may have slowed the rate of fire, but at least they could still fight. When bagged charges were loaded and rammed into the chamber the paper or linen wrapping had to be pierced in order to expose the propellant. This was done by the gunner inserting a fine spike, known either as a 'pricker' or 'priming iron', down the vent hole to break the covering. When the fine priming powder was then poured into the vent, this would trickle down the vent hole and form a continuous burning train to ignite the bagged charge when the portfire or slow match on the linstock was applied. Eventually bagged charges would be taken a stage further, and the projectile attached to the bag by means of securing straps. This reduced the time taken to load, because only one object had to be handled, rather than two.

The artillery train was moved by the gunners and their assistants. It was a slow and laborious method of moving the guns and ammunition. This is a recreated scene, but is representative of how the gunners must have worked to move the artillery.

THE ARTILLERY TRAIN

In his work *A Light to the Art of Gunnery*, published in 1689, Captain Thomas Binning vividly describes the preparation of an artillery train for the march, and all its tools and accompanying attendants. He talks of 'the Order and Necessaries for Guns to march by Land, they having six demi-cannons, six Sakers or Demi-culverings, with two Whole-cannons, besides the Field Ordnance'. He then goes on to record how the role of the pioneers attached to the artillery was to prepare the road it was due to pass along, and either repair the surface or strengthen any bridges. For this purpose the workforce were equipped with picks, shovels and crowbars, along with other implements. Binning continues to describe how after the pioneers had completed their work, the artillery train followed: 'After them first follow the 6 Sakers or Demi-culverings with their Provision of Ball in Wagons.'

In the event that a gun capsized or swerved off the road, then a labour force, known as harbingers, accompanied the train, to recover such a weapon and keep the column on the move. The duties of these men also included the greasing of axles, and ensuring the towing ropes, known as 'prolonges' in France, were

Method of hauling the gun muzzle first using manual labour. The carriage trail drags on the ground and attendants are guiding the wheels as the weapon is moved.

properly attached to the wagons and guns. The lighter equipment brought up the rear of the artillery train, and Binning notes this as comprising 'the Carriage of Ladles, Sponges, and Rammers, Match, Crows and Handspikes, and Budg-barrels.' This last item, sometimes written as 'budge-barrel', was an essential: a wooden barrel containing leather sacks filled with gunpowder, and fitted with copper hoops and nails. This kept the powder dry and prevented accidental spillage.

A train of artillery could stretch out to cover several miles of road, and could take many hours to pass a single point. Large trains could extend for fifteen miles (24km) or more, and the damage caused to roads by its passing was enormous. The draught animals to haul the guns were either horses or oxen, each of which had their own merits. Horses, Binning calculated, were capable of hauling 350lb (160kg) of metal, and were fast, but lacked endurance. He had originally believed horses capable of hauling 500lb metal per gun (227g). He realized the benefits of oxen and wrote: 'If you order a Yoke of Oxen for a Horse Draught, it will be equal.' Naturally oxen were slower animals, but they had greater endurance and strength, plus the men were not so reluctant to eat them in an emergency. However, it should be pointed out that oxen used as draught animals would only be eaten as a last resort, otherwise the wagons and artillery could not move.

Men could haul the guns, and Thomas Binning calculated that on a good road it would take thirty men to pull a gun weighing 3,000lb (1,360kg), allowing that each man could pull 100lb (4.5kg) of metal. On an average road

Using horses to haul artillery muzzle first. Artillery continued to be moved in this manner until quite late in the seventeenth century.

this capability dropped to 80lb (36kg) of metal to be towed by a man, which meant that it required thirty-seven or thirty-eight men to pull a gun weighing 3,000lb. Binning may have been over-optimistic, because forty-seven years earlier Captain Henry Hexham had computed more realistic figures relating to haulage capacities.

In his book P*rinciples of the Art Military Practised in the Warres of the United Netherlands*, published in Delft in Holland circa 1642, Captain Henry Hexham wrote of his observations concerning artillery trains from actual experience in war. Within this work the author mentions how small punts or boats should be included in the train so that the artillery could be transported over rivers where there is no bridge. This is probably something that he experienced during his service in Holland, where the land is low-lying and prone to flooding. However, it did serve to highlight that an artillery train should be self-contained to allow the men in attendance to deal with any contingency. Hexham mentions that it should be possible to form its own defence and move the train into blocks or 'squares' to fight off any attack by cavalry. He mentions the usefulness of wagons fitted with four wheels, which provided better manoeuvrability. Among his observations he notes:

> '...through Moorish, foule, and sandie ways upon this because the peece lieth more steddie, and is not subject to so much

Bronze cannon of the seventeenth-century period. Note the lifting handles, referred to as 'dolphins', and length of barrel, which is of cast bronze.

> wrenching aside in durtie and ruttie waies, than upon its proper carriage. Now whensoever an Enemie should draw near unto an Armie by the help of the Fearne you may quickly hoize it up and lay it upon its own carriage'.

What Hexham is telling us here, is that for ease of transport the barrels of certain weapons were removed from their usual gun carriage and placed on wagons fitted with four wheels, in order to improve the marching speed and manoeuvrability. The device to which he refers as the fearne is a type of basic 'A'-framed crane, which would be used to lift the barrel of the gun on to its carriage in preparation for battle. Such a tactic eased the burden on the march, but could increase the preparation time in deploying for battle. Equipment such as the fearne crane had been illustrated in the works of Leonardo da Vinci, whose sketches show such devices being used to lift barrels of artillery pieces. Each gunner had his own particular observations and personal opinions, having encountered a unique range of difficulties.

The true mark of genius was the master gunner's ability to bring about a solution to any obstacle or difficulty that the artillery train might encounter whilst on the march: in other words, he had to be prepared for the unexpected at every stage. Improvisation was often called for, such as during the Monmouth Rebellion in England during 1685. At the Battle of Sedgemore on 6 July 1685 the royal artillery train was so lacking in horses that the coach horses of the Bishop of Winchester were commandeered to haul the guns. At the same battle there was such a lack of trained gunners in the king's artillery force that Sergeant Weems of Dumbarton's Regiment served the guns. Such actions kept the artillery serviceable, and it also prevented the possibility of the rebellion spreading, and safeguarded the throne of England.

AMMUNITION

The Cannon Ball

The main type of projectile fired by the guns was the solid cast-iron ball or 'round shot' of varying weight. There were still some older weapons to be found that fired stone balls, known as petrieroes (stone throwers), but they lacked the striking power of artillery and were not so destructive. Besides, to produce projectiles for these weapons required the skills of a

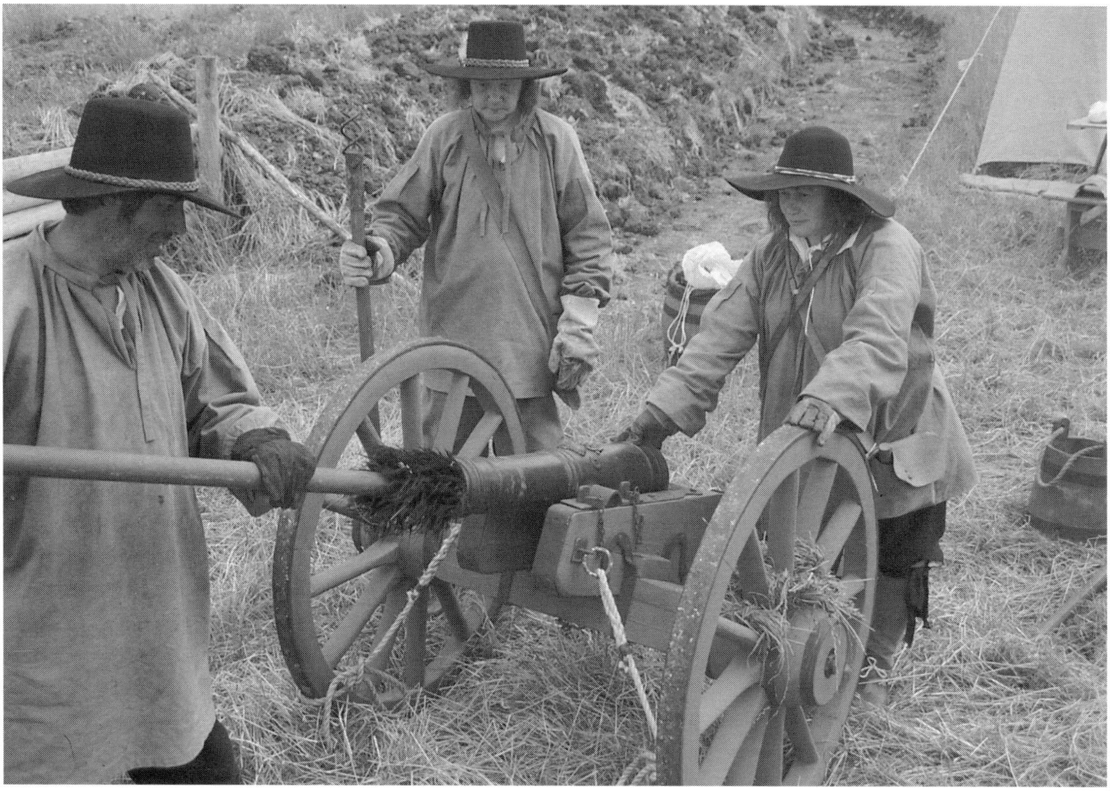

Gunners loading a piece of artillery known as a minion extraordinaire, a non-standard weapon. The recreated scene shows gunners using a range of items associated with loading the gun. Note the wooden bucket containing water used to swab out the barrel between shots.

stone mason to shape the stone into a perfect sphere. The iron ball was easier and quicker to produce, and size for size, in relation to stone, had a much denser weight, which produced greater damage on striking the target.

Iron balls were used by artillery at sea and on land. The French referred to these as 'rond', meaning round, and it is from this expression that it is believed we derive the term 'round' to identify a single projectile of ammunition. In fact the noun 'ammunition' is also derived from the French term 'la munition'. When these projectiles were fired by land artillery, great shards of stones were thrown up by the impact, and iron balls could often be seen bouncing across the battlefield because of their low muzzle velocity. These would often carry out to ranges of 800 to 1,500yd (730 to 1,370km), and tear into the massed ranks of the infantry, which they destroyed with crushing effect. Even when the main force of these projectiles had been expended, they still presented great danger as they rolled harmlessly, or so it would seem, across the battlefield; many a man lost a foot or complete leg as he indulgently tried to stop the progress of a very heavy object that was still travelling deceptively fast. Against brick

Cavalry charges were vulnerable to artillery fire, but were necessary to try and break the enemy's ranks.

and stone walls these iron balls would create a deadly wounding effect, as heavy stone fragments flew off under the weight of the impact. Against the wooden hulls of ships at sea they produced large wooden splinters that, like the stone shards, inflicted horrendous wounds.

In addition to these standard projectiles there was a range of specialized ammunition designed to create maximum damage against specific targets. At sea such projectiles included chain and expanding bar shot to destroy the rigging of an enemy ship and render it immobile (*see* Chapter 9, Naval Artillery).

Canister Shot

Among the range of special ammunition for use by artillery on land the most deadly was the type known as either canister or case shot. This comprised a thin sheet of metal bent into a cylinder and nailed to a wooden disc. Loaded into this was a payload of broken nails and other small pieces of scrap iron or, for a more consistent wounding effect, dozens of musket balls. This was then capped off by a lid that kept the contents in place. On firing, the thin metal casing burst, and the numerous small projectiles were released as a hail of shot that spread out to produce deadly wounds. Canister projectiles were loaded in the same manner as iron balls, but their use was reserved until the enemy infantry was at close range of only 300yd (274m). The effect at such close quarters was devastating, and against cavalry charges canister shot was guaranteed to halt all but the most determined attacks.

Incendiary Shells

For use against buildings the artillery could use heated shot, in the hope that it would cause the timbers of buildings to catch alight. Heated shot was simply cast-iron shot heated in a brazier until it was white hot. It was then transferred to the cannon in a special cradle-like carrier where it was loaded. To separate the ball from the propellant charge of gunpowder and prevent premature ignition, the gunners would insert a disc, called a tompion, made from green wood to act as the wad instead of the usual straw or rope. The gun crew had to work fast, but the effect would invariably produce results. At sea a similar practice was also used, but seamen were understandably nervous about using heated shot because of the risk of causing accidental fire on board their own ship. The use of heated shot can actually be traced back to the time of Stephen Bathori, the king of Poland, who is believed to be the first person to order its use during the war against Russia in 1579.

True incendiary shells, called carcasses, were introduced around 1672 and were a much safer option than heated shot. The invention of the carcass is credited to Christopher van Galen, the Prince Bishop of Munster. There is reason to believe he may have been influenced by a similar device invented by Master Gunner Samuel Zimmerman in 1573. The carcass was a hollow shell formed into spirals from strips of metal to produce an egg-like shape. The incendiary mixture was highly inflammable and made up of turpentine, resin, saltpetre, sulphur, antimony and tallow. According to references the carcasses did not have a very predictable or stable trajectory, and the round version had a tendency to detonate on being fired. Despite this, the carcass was a useful type of ammunition. The intensity with which it must have burned would have made it virtually impossible to extinguish. With regard to accuracy, when used against a town or city this did not matter unduly because it would have been the randomness of their landing which would have caused fear and confusion among the defenders. The carcass was taken into service by many armies, including the English army which used them to set fire to the city of Limerick during the siege of 1690.

There is a certain confusion over the term 'carcass'. Some historians refer to carcasses as being discharged from mortars, but they appear to have misinterpreted the term and believe it to mean the bodies of dead animals or humans. This confusion is quite understandable, but is compounded when they continue by claiming that sewage was also fired from artillery, and mortars in particular. For example, the historian Peter Morton in an essay on seventeenth-century artillery claims that during the English Civil War mortars were used to fire sewage and carcasses at targets to 'add to the discomfort of the defenders'. However, anyone who understands the explosive forces involved in firing artillery will realize that this is impossible. The soft body tissue of a carcass, animal or human, would quite literally be torn apart by the force of the propellant. With sewage we are asked to believe that a load comprising largely of liquid is fired in the same manner as an iron ball. Even if this effluent were loaded into a container, the force on firing would throw the sewage everywhere, because artillery cannot fire liquid in the same way as a solid projectile.

Mortar Shells

The last category of projectile to be fired by artillery at this time was the mortar. This type

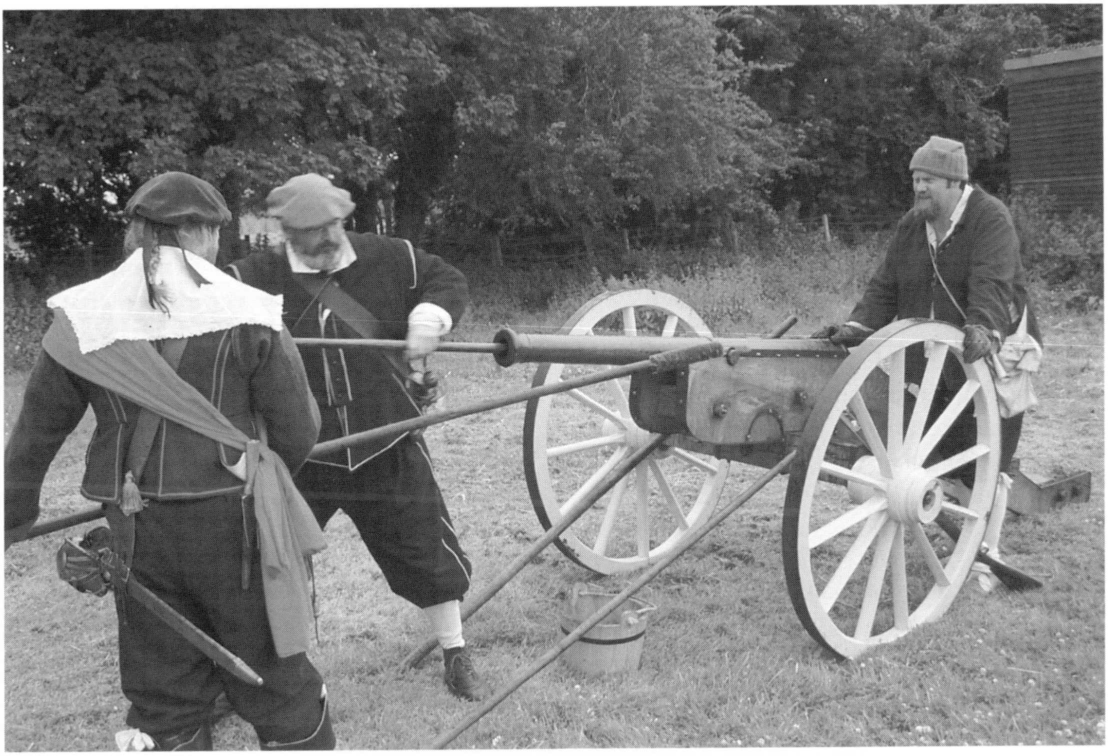

Recreated scene showing how the gunners used rammers to load artillery such as this falconet.

of ammunition is referred to as being either a shell or bomb, and could weigh from as little as 5lb (2.2kg), to extraordinarily large calibres of 450lb (204kg). These were fired at close range and aimed so as to project the shell in a high angle of trajectory in order to lob the shell over walls. The mortar shell was just that: a hollow sphere that served as a shell to contain a charge of gunpowder. The term is believed to originate from the German word schale, which means 'outer rind or bark'. The shell was designed to explode inside the confines of a town or city under siege, and this was achieved by using a fuse to detonate the gunpowder charge contained within the projectile.

This was a point of great contention, with some gunners advocating lighting the fuse before firing the weapon, and others believing that if the fuse was set to face the main propellant charge, then the flash from the blast would ignite the fuse. The main argument seems to be over the burning time of the fuse. If it were cut too long the shell would land before detonating and the defenders stood a chance of extinguishing the fuse before it detonated. Cut too short and the shell could detonate before even reaching the target. Another drawback was the possibility that the shell could explode inside the mortar, with all the resultant consequences. By exercising good judgement an experienced gunner could cut the correct length of fuse which would detonate the shell at the optimum moment to cause the greatest damage and even cause fires to be ignited.

In some armies the shell was called a 'granado' and the hollow sphere filled with 'wild fire' or 'fire works', in order to produce an incendiary effect when the shell exploded. The mortar shells were filled with their explosive contents by experienced gunners or others familiar with such work, having previously made hand grenades. Instructions on how to fill mortar shells includes one formula which calls for three parts of gunpowder: '...well pounded and sifted, Greekish pitch (one third), and halfe the weight thereof in brimstone (sulphur)'. The instructions continue by mentioning the fact that the mixture or compound can be 'supplemented' by adding one half part of ordinary salt and mixing: '...well together, with oyle of linseed'. This would have produced intense heat when detonated and the incendiary effect to buildings would have been great. The blast and fragments of the shell casing when it exploded would have killed or severely wounded anyone standing within the radius of its blast.

The usefulness of the shell was realized, and it was introduced as a projectile for use from field artillery. This would become referred to as the 'common shell' and was usually fused to explode over the heads of advancing infantry between ranges of 300 and 800 yards. Larges pieces of metal from the deflagrating shell would be propelled in all directions, causing widespread injuries. This early form of anti-personnel ammunition could decimate the ranks of infantry and cavalry and cause confusion. Later on other projectiles with better fusing would be introduced and these would have a more deadly anti-personnel effect. Another type of projectile was designed for the mortar, and this was oval in shape as opposed to being round. It is to this projectile that the term 'bomb' was applied, but in use it was fused and fired in the same way as the more conventional mortar shell.

IN CONCLUSION

This range of ammunition and specialized tolls for the artillery would remain virtually unchanged for the next 200 years. Some new introductions would be made, but for the most part this was what the artillery would have in service. However, it was the way in which the guns were used in battle, and the size to which they developed, with increased projectile size, that would determine the outcome of an engagement.

11 The Gunners and Printed Books

During the seventeenth century printed works on the subject of artillery were becoming more commonplace. However, not all master gunners approved, because they believed that such works would undermine their position as more people learned about artillery through the printed word. The generally accepted method of passing on the required skills for gunners was by word of mouth, and some master gunners felt strongly that the distribution of books on the subject of artillery would herald the end of their professional standing among fighting units. They were primarily concerned that previously undisclosed facts governing the art of gunnery would be available to all who could read – although the fact that a great many of these books of instruction were actually written by master gunners seems to fly in the face of such a belief.

THE WRITTEN WORD VERSUS WORD OF MOUTH

The authors of books on the use of artillery were no doubt writing down their knowledge in the hope that by doing so such information would not be lost. After all, there is only so much detail that a man can commit to memory, and sometimes facts can become distorted. However, with a written work as a reference source to clarify any discrepancy concerning, say, loading the correct charge of gunpowder, the gunner could check with a guideline chart in the book. But books were very expensive and some were large volumes, and they were not necessarily as widely available as some master gunners feared. For the reason of cost alone books would only be acquired by those who could afford them, and this tended to be the aristocracy who would have had the education enabling them to read and understand such works.

Books and other written pamphlets on the matter of artillery had been appearing for some time, but for those who did not have the literacy skills to fully understand the written word, such published works were meaningless. Therefore gunners still preferred to pass on their secrets by word of mouth, and then only when they believed their protégés were ready and worthy to receive such information; experience had taught master gunners many lessons in artillery through trial and error. It was also essential that master gunners not only knew how to read and write, but, just as importantly, understood mathematics in order to work out the weights and ratios for the safe and effective operation of artillery; this was where the printed chart was essential as an *aide memoire* that was always kept ready to hand.

Because of the increasing importance of learning these literacy skills, by 1620 the number of gunners who fully appreciated and understood the works of such people as Nicolo Fontana Tartaglia was on the increase. This readership admired the achievements of

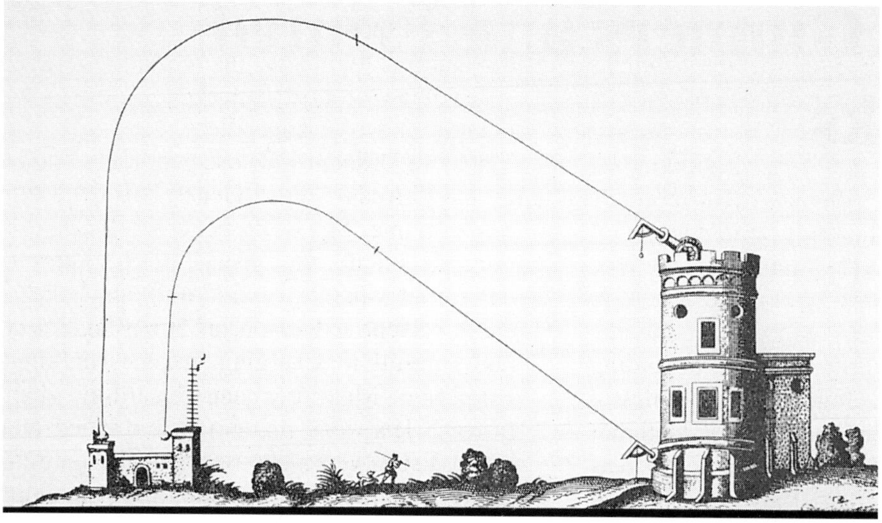

Illustration from a seventeenth-century work showing the use of the gunner's quadrant. The text would expand on the use of this device.

Gun positions as illustrated in a seventeenth-century work showing the ideal layout for a battery.

Tartaglia, a self-taught scientific writer and military theorist, who, through his own experiments, and his work in developing such items as the gunners' quadrant, had done much to advance the science of gunnery. Tartaglia's theories were now being applied directly to the actual use of artillery in warfare, and whilst many remained of great use, a number were improved. As an author on military matters, Tartaglia had written down his findings in a three-volume series of books entitled *Colloques Concerning the Arte of Shooting*, which joined his work Nuova Scientia that had appeared in 1537. This was one of the first works of its kind to examine military tactics in depth, and to formulate theories on defences and make suggestions for improvements.

By the seventeenth century, books covering all aspects of warfare were beginning to appear. These were volumes of instructions intended to pass on the skills required by gunners, and to assist in the training of soldiers. Such works would have been of great help to non-military men who, due to circumstances, found themselves thrust into commanding troops in battle. For example, Oliver Cromwell had no formal training as a military commander, being by turn deeply religious, a farmer and politician, but he emerged as a natural leader and tactician during the English Civil War. No doubt as an educated man he would have either read or known something about such works as *The Five Decades and Epistles of Warre* written by Francis Markham and published in London by Augustine Matthews in 1622. At the time his work was published, Markham was fifty-seven years old and had been a professional soldier, having seen service in Flanders and Holland. Therefore, his writings held substance and were based directly on his experiences and his ideas on how he thought best to improve the military.

Markham was particularly concerned with the use and role of artillery, especially the Master of Ordnance, whose position is sometimes referred to as the 'General of Artillery'. For example, Markham believed that junior gunners should be supervised in order to determine whether or not they were sufficiently adept at the job, and 'skilful, ready and carefull in Charging and Discharging, Levelling, Mounting and Guarding their peeces'. His work was most comprehensive, and it also covered the use of artillery at sea, the weight and transportation of artillery pieces, and how the guns should be sited and deployed on the battlefield. Such concise works proved invaluable to military and non-military men alike.

THE VALUE OF THE WRITTEN WORD

The question does arise that if all military men were reading such books, then all the

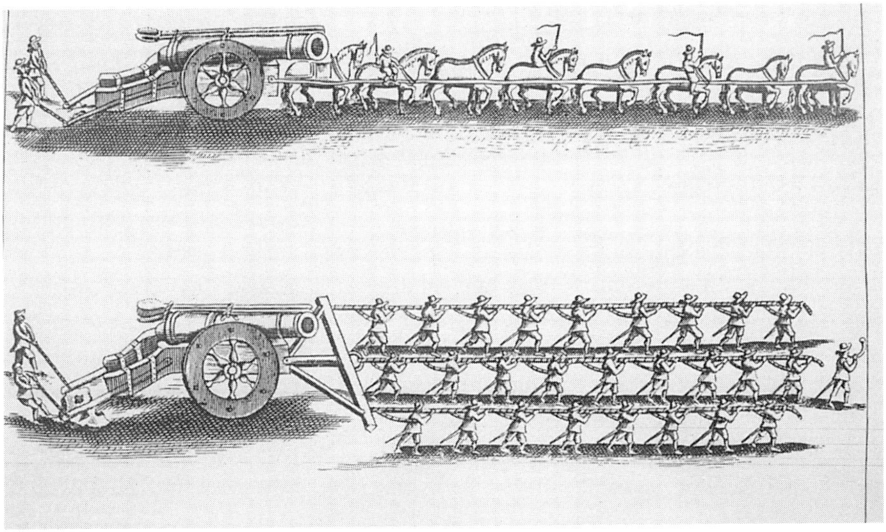

Method of hauling artillery as illustrated in a seventeenth-century work, showing horses compared to manpower.

tactics employed would be the same, and the opposing forces would mirror each other's disposition on the battlefield. There is certainly an element of risk that such a situation could arise. However, not everybody disseminates the written word in exactly the same way, and this is where variation on a theme emerges: for example, one person may read a suggestion and take it at face value, while another may read the same passage and find flaws in the suggestion and alter the findings to suit his own purpose. The use of artillery on the battlefield may, therefore, be likened to a game of chess: the pieces may be the same, but it is how the individual chooses to use them that decides the outcome of an engagement, which in warfare is a battle governed by artillery. Books made people think, and this in turn led to continued improvement in artillery and the way in which it was used.

Books such as *The Art of Gunnery*, written in 1627, served to dispel a great many of the myths surrounding the use of gunpowder. Without doubt it was a very dangerous substance, but even in the seventeenth century some gunners were superstitious enough still to be expounding theories and beliefs that rational people had long since consigned to the list of rumours and legends that were linked to the use of artillery. For example, one particular work, *Shewing the Properties Office and Duties of a Gunner* by Cyprian Lucar, recommended that:

> Every Gunner ought to know that as it is a wholesome thing for him to drink and eat a little meat before he doth discharge any piece of ordnance, because the fume of saltpetre and brimstone will otherwise be hurtful to his brains, so it is very unwholesome for him to shoot any piece of ordnance while his stomach is full…

This may seem to be utter nonsense because, hungry or satiated, the guns still had to be fired when ordered. The same work does, however, contain more serious points: for instance, it suggests that a gunner prepare his gunpowder charges of even weight in cloth bags, known as cartridges, before a battle, instead of having to scoop it into the barrel with a wooden ladle in the midst of battle. Such a move ensured a more standard charge, and did away with the gunner having to estimate the load with rough calculation in the thick of fighting.

WHERE BOOKS FALL SHORT

Through various writings artillerymen were made more aware of the problems in handling gunpowder, and in particular the dangers involved in loading a gun with a charge too powerful for the weapon. Books contained a wealth of useful advice, but there was still much that authors did not understand, such as why certain things happened when they did. For example, they could explain that if the 'air was thick or thinne' (atmospheric pressure and precipitation) the cannon ball would travel to either greater or shorter distances. Likewise, if the wheels of the gun carriage were not properly levelled the barrel would be canted and the shot would not hit the intended target.

Some gunners had experience built up from many years of observation, but they could still not explain with any great lucidity certain actions and reactions between a charge of gunpowder and the projectile. Indeed, the trajectory of a projectile was another phenomenon for which they had no ready answer. Tartaglia had written of his observations in the sixteenth century that: 'A peece of artillery cannot shoot one pace in a straight lyne.' However, he did realize that the greater the velocity of a projectile, the flatter its trajectory, and recorded: 'the more swift the pellet doth fly, the less crooked is its range'. This was because a more powerful charge of gunpowder was used, and its penetrative capabilities were therefore improved, though unfortunately that was not realized at the time. However, it was known that if the barrel of a gun were elevated to an angle of 45 degrees, and loaded with the correct charge, then it could fire a projectile to its maximum range.

All of these observations were being recorded in book form, from which others could learn and, through experiments, even improve on.

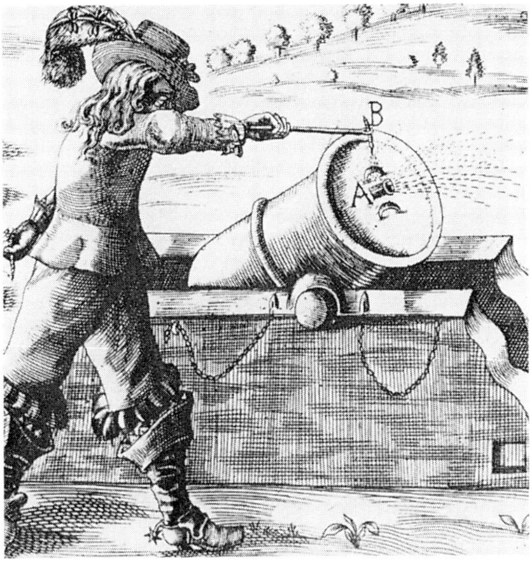

An illustration from a military manual, circa *seventeenth century, showing how a mortar was operated. The gunner is igniting the fuse of the mortar bomb.*

THE ROLE OF BOOKS IN TRAINING

As the century progressed, so more works appeared, such as *Military Discipline: or the Young Artilleryman*, written by Barriffe in 1635. In his work he states:

> The first Rudiments of educations, wherewithall to enter young Souldiers… ought to be the well managing of their Armes, which may easily be attained by frequent Practice, and the Souldiers thereby be brought to use them with ease, safety and delight.

In other words, the author is emphasising the need for proper training and practice, something that would produce a reliable infantryman or artilleryman. Rather than it being disastrous for artillery or any other branch of the army, for that matter, books were to lead to a better understanding of guns and their tactical use, in what was fast becoming the real force on the battlefield.

One example of how an acute shortage of properly trained gunners could hamper operations became evident during the siege of Limerick in Ireland between May and June in 1642. The English Civil War had erupted and fighting had spread to Ireland, with the Royalist and Parliamentarian armies despatching men to the country. During the siege artillery was deployed in an effort to reduce the stronghold, but it became obvious that the gunners lacked training and experience. Artillery fire was directed at houses to prevent the city's defenders from seeking shelter, but in their efforts to produce results the artillerymen became overzealous and loaded charges of gunpowder that were too powerful for the guns.

The problem of overloading pieces of artillery was known to be the result of a lack of proper training, and represented a dangerous problem on the battlefield. One such incident occurred during the siege when a piece of

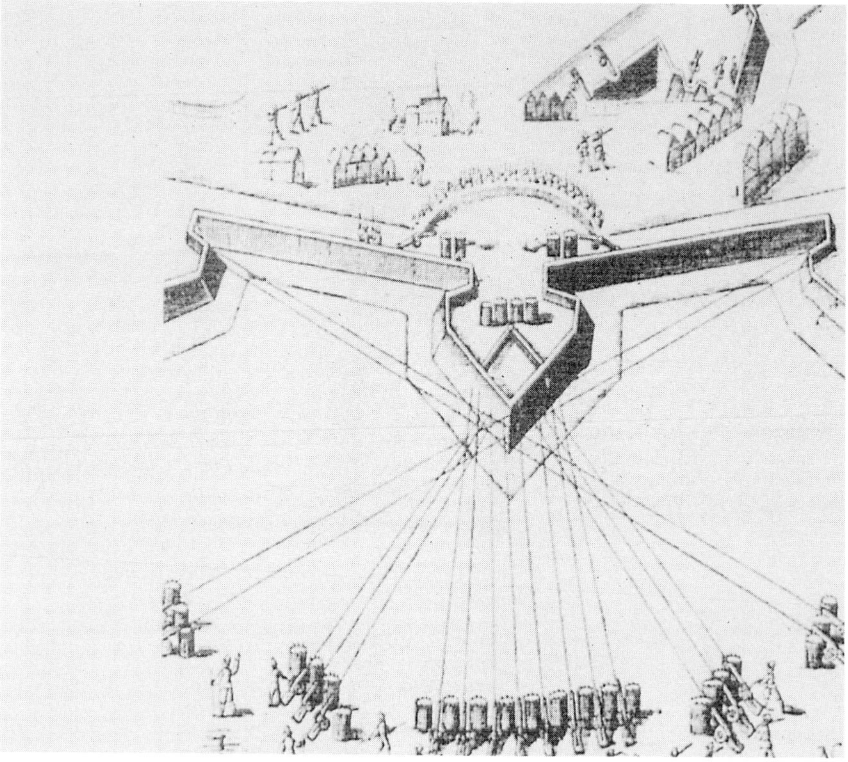

Illustration from a manual showing how artillery could be directed against the defensive walls of a town. The guns are concentrating on one particular point in order to break through and allow the infantry to attack.

artillery accidentally blew up, killing Master Gunner Beech and the entire gun crew. This further highlighted how inexperienced some gun crews actually were at the time, a problem that could only be resolved by training. Further, the solution would only come about as books revealing the military thinking of the age, especially that governing artillery, became more widely disseminated – for instance, such works as *The Principles of the Art Militaire*, published circa 1643. Problems in gunnery would remain with both sides during the English Civil War – and even when the New Model Army was raised in 1645, artillery was still low on the list of priorities. In an effort to remedy the shortage of trained gunners and correct the ignorance among those with experience, manuals such as William Eldred's *The Gunner's Glass* were published, the latter in England in 1647.

Across Europe a range of new titles was beginning to appear, some of which contained completely original material and were supported by highly technical instructions and illustrations. Other works were no more than reiterations of earlier writings, containing all the errors without any attempt at correcting them. Eventually authors emerged such as Sir Jonas Moore, who, in 1673, published *Modern Fortification; or Elements of Military Architecture*, a work that examined the way in which barrels were manufactured, and the calibres of artillery and their usefulness. His work was complemented in 1689 with the appearance of *A Light to the Art of Gunnery* written by Captain Thomas

Illustration from a book circa *1670 showing how artillery should be used against walled towns in order to breech the defences.*

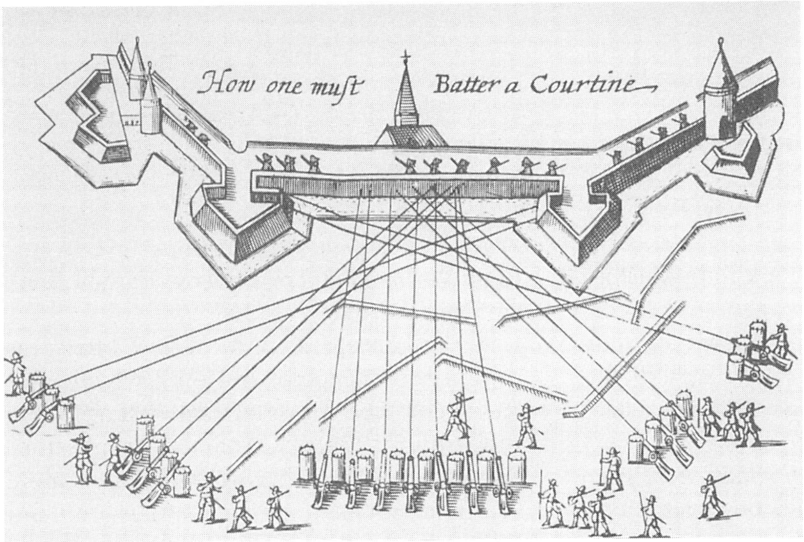

Detail of artillery positions showing gunners firing against the walls of a city. Note the mortars being prepared for firing, with the crews protected by gabions filled with earth.

Binning, and between these two works many matters were set right. These books were but two titles among many which would continue to be the mainstay of passing on details of a branch of arms that was becoming ever more increasingly complicated. As the late historian and author on artillery Ian V. Hogg put it: '…numerous books available on the art and science of gunnery, and "natural philosophers", were beginning to make a serious study of the flight of shot or, at least, as serious a study as their knowledge allowed'.

Bibliography

Bull, Stephen *An Historical Guide to Arms and Armour* Studio Editions 1991.

Brice, Martin *Forts and Fortresses* Quarto Publishing 1990.

Brown, G.I. *The Big Bang; A History of Explosives* Sutton 1998.

Chandler, David *The Art of Warfare on Land* Hamlyn 1974.

Carver, Field Marshal Lord *The Seven Ages of the British Army* Grafton 1986.

Cleator, P.E. *Weapons of War* Robert Hale 1967.

Comparato, Frank *The Age of the Great Guns* Stackpole Books 1965.

Davies, John *A History of Wales* Penguin 1990.

Ffoulkes, Charles *Arms and Armament* Harrap 1945.

Fuller, J.F.C. *The Decisive Battles of the Western World 480BC–1757* Paladin 1970.

Haythornthwaite, Philip *The English Civil War* Blandford Press 1983.

Hogg, Brigadier O.F.G *English Artillery 1326–1716* Royal Artillery Institution 1963.

Hogg, Ian V. *Fortress – A History of Military Defence* MacDonald and Jane's 1975.

Hogg, Ian V. *A History of Artillery* Hamlyn 1974.

Keegan, John *A History of Warfare* Pimlico 1994.

Koch, H.W. *History of Warfare* Bison 1987.

Lempriere, Raoul *Portrait of the Channel Islands* Robert Hale 1970.

Longmate, *Norman Island Fortress; The Defence of Great Britain 1603–1945* Collins 1991.

Macksey, Kenneth *Guinness History of Land Warfare* Guinness 1973.

Montgomery of Alamein, Field Marshal Lord *A History of Warfare* Collins 1968.

Norris, John *Artillery, A History* Sutton 2000.

O'Connell, Robert *Of Arms and Men* Oxford University Press 1989.

Peterson, Harold *The Book of the Gun* Hamlyn 1970.

Pope, Dudley *Guns* Spring Books 1969.

Reid, William *The Lore of Arms* Purnell Book Services 1976.

Rogers, Colonel H.C.B. *Artillery Through the Ages* Military Book Society 1971.

Rybot, N.V.L. *Gorey Castle* The Société Jersiaise 1978.

Rybot, N.V.L. *Elizabeth Castle* The Société Jersiaise 1986.

Wilkinson, Frederick *The World's Great Guns* Hamlyn 1977.

Woolrych, Austin *Battles of the English Civil War* Pimlico 1991.

Index

Adolphus, Gustavus (King of Sweden) 7, 9, 19 20, 21, 22–33, 44
Alberquerque, Matias 25
ammunition types *see* grapes, canister, ball
ammunition, effect of 80, 120, 143–148
artillery parks 9
artillery train *see* train
Augsburg, War of the League of 58–62
Azov Campaign 75

Bacon, Roger 137
bagged charges 137–139
Bank of England 41
barrel casting 100–109
Barriffe 153
Batten, Admiral William 113
Batten's fleet list 114–115
battles:
Aughrim (1691) 59
Beachy Head (1690) 61
Bhat-Le (1633) 67
Bothwell Bridge (1679) 55
Braddock Down (1643) 79
Breitenfield (1631) 7, 27, 28, 29–30
Colby Heath (1645) 87
Dunes (1658) 118
Edgehill (1642) 77, 78, 80
Fleurus (1690) 61
Honigfeld (1629) 24
Jankau (1645) 33
Klushino (1610) 73
La Hogue (Barfleur) (1691) 60
Lostwithiel (1644) 84
Lutzen (1632) 30–33
Marston Moor (1644) 79
Montijo (1644) 25
Nagashino 1575) 70
Nordlingen (1634) 26, 33
Preston (1648) 82, 82
Riga (1656) 75
Roundway Down (1643) 79
Rowton Heath (1646) 83
Scheveningen (1653) 117
Sedgemore (1688) 55
Seki-ga-Hara (1600) 69
Staffarda (1690) 61
Truong-duc (1633) 67
Baud, Peter 106
bayonet 50
Beech, Master Gunner 154
Bethune, De Henry 10–11
Bethune, Maximilian de (Duc de Sully) 101
Binning, Thomas 43–44, 53, 54, 140, 141, 154
Bird, Sir William 14
Biringguccio, Vannoccio 104
blast furnace 17
books of instruction 149–155
Boufflers, Duke Louis de 4
Bourne, William 113
Brown, George 103, 110

Caerphilly Castles, Wales 86
carriage, gun 54, 107
case shot (canister) 80, 145

Castle Cornet (Guernsey) 50, 99
Channel Islands 50–52, 97–99; *see also* Jersey and Guernsey
Chapman, Jasper 13
Charles I, King of England 77–99
Charles II, King of England 99
Charles IX, King of Sweden 19
China 66
Christian IV King of Denmark 35
Churchill, John 55
Clerville, Chevalier de 37
Clinometer 49, 50
clocks *see* timepieces
Coehoorn, Menno van 40–42
Comminge 42
Conde, Prince of 36–37
Conway, Sir Edward 14
Cromwell, Oliver 7, 79, 82–83, 85, 102, 103, 110, 117, 151

Danzig 50
Deal Castle 93, 128, 129
Denbigh, Earl of 78
Dhool Dhanee 67
Dieppe 61
Donnington Castle 86
Douai school for infantry 44
dragoons 64–65
drill for loading guns 129–131

Eldred, William 129, 132–133, 154
Elizabeth Castle (Jersey) 13–14, 97–98
Elizabeth I, Queen of England 11
English Civil War 77–99

Ferdinand, Archduke 22
Feversham, Earl of 55
Ffoley, Thomas 103, 110
Frond, War of 36
fusiliers regiment raised 63–65, 64

gabions 34
Glencoe massacre 58
Gonzales, Antonio 50
Gordon, General Patrick 74
grape shot 30
Grotius, Edward 16
Guernsey 50–52
gun crew on ship 122–123
gun drill see drill
gunpowder 137–139

hacks 54
Henry IV King of France 10
Hexham, Captain Henry 142–143
Hideyoshi, Toyomoti 68–72
Holk, Henry 32
Horn, General Gustavus 33
horses 54
Hounslow Camp 56
howitzer 62, 63

Ieyasu, Minomoto 69–72
Ieyasu, Takugawa 69–72
incendiary shell 146
Ireland 58–62

Jacobties 58, 59
James I, King of England 11, 12, 19, 22
James II, King of England 55–57
James VI, of Scotland 11
Japan 46, 47, 66, 68–72
Jersey 13, 14, 52

Kalter guns *see* leather guns
ketch, bomb 124
Kremlin 74

Le Havre 61
Leake, Captain John 58
Leake, Captain Richard (Master Gunner) 16
leather guns 21, 26, 28
Legge, Colonel George 50, 52
Linstock 134, 135
Louis XIV King of France 11, 41, 44, 58, 60

Louvois, Marquis de see Tillier
Lucar, Cyprian 152
Malta, defences 59, 60, 62
Manchu 66
Markham, Francis 121, 151
Marlborough, Duke of 42
Maximilian of Bavaria 30–33
Mazarin, Cardinal 37
Monck, General George 117
Monmouth, Duke of 55–56
Monmouth Rebellion 1688 55–56
Monroe, Robert 29
Mont Orgueil Castle (Jersey) 14, 16, 15
Moolk-I-Meidan 66, 67
Moore, Sir Jonas 48, 120, 124, 154–155
mortar shells 146–148
mortars 42–44, 124, 153
Moscow 73, 101
Munster, Treaty of 33

Nantes, Edict of 60
Nassau, John of 16
Nassau, Maurice of 21
New Model Army 83–85, 127, 154
Norton, Robert 78

Osnabruck, Treaty of 33
Oxensterna, Axel 26

Pappenheim, Count Gottfried zu 28, 30–33
partridge (mortar) 42
Pembroke Castle, Wales 87
Pepys, Samuel 108
Perriers 47
Perry, Commodore Matthew 72
petard 20
Peter the Great, Tsar of Russia 75, 76
Pett, Phineas 112
Plymouth defences 61
portfire 134
Portugal 25–26

quadrant, gunner's 49, 50 136–137, 150

Raglan Castle, Wales 35–36
Raleigh, Sir Walter 14
rammer for loading see tools
recoil on firing 121
Richelieu, Cardinal 36
rifling 35
Rooke, Admiral George 60
Russell, Admiral Edward 60
Russia 73–76
Ruyter, Michiel de 126
Ryswick, Treaty of 62

Samurai warriors (Japan) 69–72
Savoy, Duke of 61
Schulenburg, Count 42, 47
Scott, Robert 22
siege tactics 38–39
sieges:
  Ath 1697 40
  Basing House 36
  Belgrade 1682 76
  Bonn 1703 42
  Chepstow Castle 1648 88–90, 95
  Elfsbourg Castle 1612 19
  Elizabeth Castle 97–98
  Limerick 1691 59
  Londonderry 57, 58
  Maastrict 1673 36
  Namur 1692 41
  Old Wardour Castle 1643 85–87
  Osaka Castle 1614–1615 70
  Pembroke Castle 94–97
  Raglan Castle 35–36, 80
Smith, Captain John 115
Smith, Sir Thomas 106
spiking the guns 38–39
swab for cleaning barrel *see* tools

Taiwan 66
Talbot, Earl Richard 58
Targalia, Niccolo 49, 103, 137, 149, 150
Tellier, Michel le 11
Thirty Years War 22, 23, 24, 26–33

Tilly, Count Johan 28, 29, 30–33
time pieces 48, 49
tools of gunner for loading 133–134
Torstensson, Lennart 7, 20, 28
Tourville, Admiral de 60
trail carriage 52, 53
trail wheel 34
train artillery 140–141

unicorn cannons 50

Vaubin, Marshal Sebastien le Prestre 36–40
Verbruggen family 105
Vinci, Leonardo da 104

Wales 87–97
Wallenstein, Count Albrecht von 30, 32, 33
Waller, Sir William 80
Weems, Sergeant 56, 143
Westphalia, Treaty of 1648 33
wildfire 148
William of Orange (King William III of England) 57, 58–62
Woolwich 16, 44, 108
worm, cleaning tool *see* tools
Wurmbrandt, Melchior 21, 22
Wurttemberg-Neustadt, Duke of 45

Zolkiewski, Hetman Stanislas 73